A Table Before Me
The Meditating Christian

David E. Ross

"Thou preparest a table before me . . . "
Psalm 23:5

"When He was at table with them,
He took the bread,
And blessed and broke it
And gave it to them.
And their eyes were opened,
And they recognized Him."
Luke 24:30-31

This book is for

Ellen

Beloved wife,
Caring mother,
Closest friend,
Meditator

This book is also dedicated to our family's next
generations of meditators:
Debbie, David, Becky
Eugene, Judy, George,
Sarah, Adrian, Dalen, Haley,
David George and Michael

And to Friends throughout the world
Who glorify God through meditating on His Word.

Acknowledgements

The writing of this book has been a long process, going back to the mid 1970's when my wife, Ellen, and I were missionaries in Korea. The reader will notice that many of the illustrations contained in this book refer to Korea. That is because our ministry has been and continues to be to the Korean people. But the principles and message of meditation are universal. I discovered that meditation on the Word of God, empowered and guided by the Holy Spirit, was the dynamic secret of effective ministry. This means that hundreds of people have contributed to the completion of this book. I would like to thank those many friends, colleagues and students who have given me insights, encouragement and challenge to write this book.

Dr. Gary Parrett, Associate Professor of Christian Education at Gordon-Conwell Theological Seminary, gave me a great and sacrificial gift of love by reading the entire manuscript and making important biblical and theological suggestions. Gary's ideas were extremely helpful to me as I completed the writing, and I would like to give him special thanks.

Dr. and Mrs. Earl W. Morey gave me an invaluable gift. Earl is a renowned Bible scholar and teacher who has taught in many nations, and he very carefully examined the manuscript and offered suggestions that helped me greatly as I completed the work. I have learned much from his deep teaching that comes out of his consecrated study and meditation on the Word of God. Betty is unsurpassed as a proofreader! I was amazed at the loving care and attention she gave to even small details in grammar, word structure and sentence structure. I must offer an apology to both Earl and Betty for causing them to work so hard, but they have my heartfelt thanks.

Thank you to Heajoung Yang for translating the book into the Korean language. Her translation is much better than the original English edition. She and Peter are loving partners in ministry.

My thanks go also to those who taught me about meditation and who enriched my life through their basic Bible teaching. I would like to thank Campbell McAlpine, who was my first and greatest teacher on meditation. Joy Dawson has taught me biblical truths that have made me stronger in my faith. Jean Darnall has taught me how to listen to the Spirit and to walk with Him in daily life. Lenna Belle Robinson, now 103 years old, is my "special mentor" in meditation. Archer and Jane Torrey, of Jesus Abbey in Korea, have been Ellen's and my greatest teachers, encouragers and models in ministry. During his lifetime, Archer "walked with the Lord," which I consider to be the essence of spirituality; and meditation on the Bible was his guide in his journey. Rev. Han Kyung Jik, of Young Nak Church in Seoul, taught me to love the Scriptures, and Professor Ronald S. Wallace, of Edinburgh, Scotland, taught me how to understand them. Rev. Park Chai Hoon taught me to worship, using the Scriptures as the basis of worship. My father in-law, Dr. T. Layton Fraser, showed me how to live in a truly biblical manner. Ron and Judy Smith, both meditators, have taught me to lay strong foundations of Bible study as I meditate.

I owe special thanks to another meditator, Stephen R. Yarnall, M.D., who has encouraged me to live life in its fullness.

I would like to thank the many students who have studied Bible meditation with me through the years. They have been my teachers.

My deepest appreciation goes to my precious wife, Ellen. Her listening ear and deep insights have made this book possible.

[In memory of Alison Oliver, October 5, 1971-
August 26, 2004
Meditator and Servant of the Lord
"Well done, good and faithful servant." Matthew 25:21]

Endorsements

"Although we have previously received and read excellent teachings on biblical meditation and put them into practice in our own personal ways, David Ross' "A Table Before Me: The Meditating Christian" has transformed and revitalized our quiet times with our Lord. This is a "fire-kindling" book! It is a "must-read" for everyone who earnestly longs for a deeper fellowship with our Lord, a clearer understanding of our faith and an energized obedience to His will. The People of God desperately need to hear and heed this message!"

Betty L. Morey
Earl W. Morey, M.Div., Ph.D.
EPC Pastor, International Evangelist & Bible Teacher

"I have waited a long time for this book. This book leads us to God. It leads us into God's Word. I was able to enter into a spiritual dialogue with the author as I read it. But soon my whole focus was on Jesus, who appeared to me in all His radiant glory."

Kang Jun Min
Pastor
Overseas Missionary Church, Los Angeles

"David has the unique ability to couple solid biblical exposition with deep spiritual experience in his ministry and teaching. This coupling is wonderfully on display in this book. My prayer is that God will use this book to draw many people nearer to Himself, and that He may do so to the building up of the Church and to the praise of His own great glory."

Gary A. Parrett
Associate Professor of Educational Ministries
Gordon-Conwell Theological Seminary

Table of Contents

Preface

To the reader:

I am so pleased to be able to offer this note of thanksgiving for the book you now hold in your hands. This
wonderful work on biblical meditation, by David Ross, is a
labor of love and a true gift to God's people.

It has been my privilege to know David and Ellen Ross
for the past twenty years. Their friendship and ministry to
me and to my family have been tremendous blessings. We
have shared fellowship on so many occasions—laughing
together, eating together, praying together, ministering
together. David's gifts of teaching and Ellen's gifts of counseling have made wonderful impacts on our souls and on the
souls of countless others. The disciples that they have raised
up through many decades of faithful ministry number in the
thousands and fill the earth.

Of particular impact to many has been David's teaching
on Bible meditation. This book is the fruit of many years of
his own teaching and, more importantly, his own practice.
One of the most striking things about the book to me as I
read it is simply knowing that David has practiced that which
he here shares with others. He is, first and foremost, one

who meditates on God's word. And God has proven himself faithful to this one who has not lived by bread alone but by every word that proceeds from the mouth of the Lord.

David has the unique ability to couple solid biblical exposition with deep spiritual experience in his ministry and teaching. This coupling is wonderfully on display in this book. While many offer sound doctrine with little personal application, and others effectively offer the reverse, David here points the reader to both. His desire is to encourage rich meditation upon the Scriptures that is built on a firm foundation of faithful interpretation, not to replace the latter with the former. Such a balanced approach is wise, essential and, sadly, all too rare.

As I read the book, my heart was both encouraged and challenged. I was encouraged by the warm and biblical vision of meditation set before me. I was challenged afresh to become one whose ear is daily awakened to hear from the God who speaks. My prayer is that God will use this book in similar and even more profound ways to draw many people nearer to Himself, and that He may do so to the building up of the Church and to the praise of His own great glory.

Amen.

Thankfully in Christ,

Gary A. Parrett
Associate Professor of Educational Ministries
Gordon-Conwell Theological Seminary
South Hamilton, Massachusetts

Psalm 139

1. O Lord, you have searched and known me.
   You know when I sit and rise.
   From afar, all thoughts discerning,
   You know where my journey lies.
   Long before I've found my own words,
   You've already heard my speech.
   All around me, you astound me!
   O, such knowledge who can reach?

2. Where could I go from Your Spirit?
   Can I from your presence flee?
   I would find you in the heavens.
   In the depths you'd surely be.
   If I flew to earth's far corners,
   Your right hand would hold me tight.
   If I tried to hide in darkness,
   You would make the darkness light.

3. In my mother's womb you formed me,
   fashioned me with greatest care.
   For such wonders I will praise you
   who beheld me even there.

In your book my days were written
Before one had come to be.
Thoughts so precious, beyond number,
Stir my soul and humble me.

4. O, that you would slay the wicked
   who defy your majesty.
   How I hate all those who hate you,
   count each one my enemy.
   Search my own heart, God, and test me.
   Know my anxious thoughts today.
   From all evil paths preserve me.
   Lead me in the ancient Way.

Gary A. Parrett, 2004

Possible Tunes:
"O the Deep, Deep Love of Jesus"
"Brethren, We Have Met to Worship"
"Come Ye Sinners, Poor and Needy"

A Word In The Beginning

The Magnetic Word

The one who reads and meditates on the Bible knows well that the Word of God is like a magnetic force. The Bible not only provides knowledge about God, it also draws the reader to itself for the purpose of *meeting* God. It has a life of its own, far more powerful, more alive, than the person approaching it. J. B. Phillips confessed, while translating the New Testament into modern, idiomatic English, that he was overwhelmed by the power of the Word of God that he was attempting to translate, feeling like an electrician working on the wiring of a house with the electricity still turned on! He found the Word of God to be more alive than he himself!

"Anyone entering the sphere of radiance of the divine word is held fast by it," remarks Hans Urs von Balthasar, "and knows from experience that this word not only communicates knowledge about God, but . . . in itself is an overpowering manifestation of God's infinity and truth, His majesty and love."[1] How true this is! We come to the Word of God thinking that we can fully understand and master that Word. Yet when God reveals Himself to us in His Word, we find rather that we are the ones who are grasped by its incredible magnetic force. We are the ones evaluated. We seek to gaze upon God in His glory, only to find that God also is gazing upon us, transforming us, drawing us unto Himself.

Consider the millions of believers who became Christians simply by reading a Gospel portion, particularly the Gospel of John. Someone witnessed to them and left a Gospel portion in their hands, or they discovered one that someone had left in a train station, or in a sports stadium. They began to read it out of curiosity but soon found themselves drawn into its magnetic field so that they had no choice other than to respond to the overwhelming presence of the living God who was waiting for them in His Word. Thus the writer of Hebrews exclaimed, "The Word of God is living and active, sharper than any two-edged sword, piercing to the division of soul and of spirit, of joints and of marrow, and discerning the thoughts and intentions of the heart!" (Hebrews 4:12)

But Jesus spoke even more directly of the life to be found in His Word: "The words that I have spoken to you are spirit and life." (John 6:63) When we meditate on Jesus' words, the Spirit who applies that Word to our hearts renews us. We then enter more fully into the abundant life promised to all followers of Christ.

As we begin our journey of meditating on the Word of God, we must know that we are meditating on the *living Word of God!* God desires to meet us daily in His Word, to speak to us as a man speaks to his friend, just as He did to Moses. (Exodus 33:11) As we come to abide in His Word, His life will become more abundant in us, His Spirit more powerful in our daily lives. We will become more truly alive! And we will taste the abundance of life in Christ; we will be satisfied in His presence. His Word will begin to rule in our lives so that we, transformed and renewed daily in His presence, become true life-givers to a world that knows only death apart from Him.

So now we begin together our journey into the heart of God, joined together by the Spirit with that great cloud of witnesses—all were meditators—who gather around the throne of the Lamb. As we start out, let us remember our chief purpose in meditating on the living Word of the Living God. Why indeed do we meditate?

We meditate because we want to meet Christ and be renewed in His presence, because we desire to hear His voice and be filled with joy at the sound.[2] We use not only our minds but also our hearts to discover who God is, so that we may "know Him more fully in order that we may love Him more deeply and follow Him more faithfully."[3] We meditate so that we can be caught up into the divine sphere of the radiance of God, and be so transformed by His Spirit that we begin to be molded into the image of Christ, the True Word of God. We then become "letters of Christ" to an unbelieving world, reflecting His image in our attitudes and relationships, and modeling His lifestyle, so that perhaps even one lost soul may see Christ within us and kneel down before Him in praise and worship.

David E. Ross
Pneuma Springs

Spirit, Church and Word

During my more than half century of pilgrimage as a Christian, I have been privileged to meet many dedicated men and women of God. But never have I met a man who walked more fully in the Spirit with as great a love for Christ and His Church, and with more commitment to serving God's people in the world, than Reuben Archer Torrey III. Father Torrey and his wife Jane founded *Jesus Abbey,* patterned after the order of Saint Benedict, deep in the mountains of Korea. Since its beginning in the early 1960's, this Anglican community has been the "heartbeat" for the great move of God's Spirit in Korea. Shortly before Father Torrey went home to be with the Lord, at age eighty-three, he was still beginning new projects, chief of which was a center to train young men and women for world evangelization. His wife Jane continues this dynamic ministry in Korea. Ellen and I are just two of the many hundreds of people who count it a privilege to have been mentored by Father Archer and Jane Torrey.

Their ministry has blessed people from around the world, and many wonder what has been the secret of such a faithful, fruitful ministry in the Lord. Surely there are many secrets: the Torreys' love for Jesus, their faithfulness to walk in the

Spirit, their compassion for His people, a life of total commitment to prayer and intercession, their life lived for the poor,
and many more. But a few years ago a young man who was
visiting asked the question directly: "Father Torrey, what is
the secret of your powerful ministry here in this mountain
community for over forty years?" Without blinking an eye,
Father Torrey immediately answered: "Meditation on the
Word of God and prayer, my young friend!" Meditation on
the Word of God! And a life of prayer that is rooted in, and
proceeds from, God's Word! This is what produces a life-
changing experience with the Living God, who will equip us
to change the world! And this is the source of the Christian's
life of fruit bearing. The psalmist tells us that the meditator is
like a "tree planted by streams of water that yields its fruit in
its season." (Psalm 1:3) The purpose of this book is to introduce you, dear reader, to the exciting privilege of meditating
on the Word of God, and to offer a few words of encouragement to speed you on your way.

Remembering Father Torrey's great sensitivity to God's
Spirit and his great love for Christ's Church, we must begin
by reminding you of the importance of allowing the Spirit
of God to lead you as you meditate and of meditating as a
member of the Universal Church—the worldwide Body of
Christ.

Spirit and Word

The first essential truth to remember is that the Spirit of
God alone enables us to receive and understand the Word of
God. He is the Spirit of Jesus who is the Eternal Word, and
of the Father who speaks the Word.

"But the anointing that you received from Him abides in
you, and you have no need that anyone should teach you,"
says John the Apostle. (1 John 2:27) The "anointing" is the
Holy Spirit dwelling and working within us, "teaching us

about everything!" The Apostle John was combating false teachers within the Church who were trying to lead people astray, so he reminded them that the Spirit of God abiding in them was teaching them directly about all that He had taught the original apostles of Jesus. Teaching His Word is one of the main ministries of the Holy Spirit, and we must *always* see the Bible and the Spirit working in unity. The Spirit always works through the Word, and the Word cannot be understood apart from the Spirit who inspired it.

Walking in the Spirit, in intimacy, holiness, obedience and humility, is the key to all meditation, as it is to all Bible study. The Bible is the "Book of the Spirit." This means that when God speaks to us, He always speaks through His Spirit. His Spirit is the Conveyor of God's truth. Human reason alone cannot understand or interpret the Word of God. Other great books can be mastered by careful study and application. The Bible cannot be mastered, but rather will always master and transform its true student.

A sign of having been filled with the Holy Spirit is a passionate hunger for the Word of God. No one who truly is controlled, or overwhelmed, by the Spirit of God will dare to offend the Spirit of God by ignoring God's Word or by approaching the Word in too casual a manner. The Spirit-filled Christian must be a Meditating Christian, for the Spirit leads us into the Word of God so that we might meet Him and hear His word to us. One of the last encouraging words Jesus promised His disciples before His crucifixion was that the Holy Spirit would reveal His Word to them. "But the Helper, the Holy Spirit, whom the Father will send in My name, He will teach you all things and bring to your remembrance all that I have said to you." Again He said, "When the Spirit of truth comes, He will guide you into all truth." (John 14:26; John 16:13)

Indeed, all Spirit-filled Christians are constrained by that Spirit to be "scholars of Christ," as George MacDonald would say. The Latin word "schola," from which we derive the word "scholar," or "school," does not mean to coldly and analytically pursue knowledge and information in order to evaluate and teach that knowledge from an exalted position. The Latin word "schola" literally means "an intermission of work," "leisure for learning," or "a meeting place for teachers and pupils." Thus, to be a "scholar" means to rest in the subject to which one directs his mind, to take time off from worldly pursuits and allow oneself to be caught up into the wonder and splendor of that which he studies. All too often Christians will approach the Scriptures from a purely academic point of view, relying on their own intellect and human strength; and the result is dead theology and human reasoning at the expense of God's truth. But when a believer walks in the Spirit, and is guided by God's Spirit, he becomes a true "Christ scholar," able then to impart the truth of the Gospel to a waiting world.

Could we not say that the central task for a theologian is to meditate on the Scriptures each morning and open himself in prayer to hear and receive all that the Spirit of God wishes to reveal to him? If students were to learn this spiritual discipline of meditation in theological seminaries, God's truth would indeed free the Church from boredom and superficiality! And we would have a living theology for the world.

Church and Word

The second essential truth to remember as we begin our journey as meditators on the Word of God, is that the Word of God always is found in the Church of the Living Christ. It is true that the Church is the fruit of the Word, yet the Church is also the "home" of the Word. God's Word comes to each individual Christian personally, but it never comes as an individual word that is separated from the community of which that believer is a part. The Christian life is life together with God and also with other believers, supernaturally bonded together in Christ, and the Word of God is the center of that community.[4] Brotherly love always flows out of true meditation.

Many Christians view the New Testament, in particular, as a purely individualistic message: we are individually saved by grace, through faith. True indeed—partially! While our salvation is personal, it is not individualistic. The four Gospels continually speak not only of our relationship to God but also of our relationship to fellow Christians and the world. Paul, throughout his letters, emphasizes reconciliation with all Christians as being central to the Christian life.

The Word comes to each one in solitude. But that solitude must be shared. And the sharing of one another's solitude, the sharing of the joy and blessings we each receive in the presence of God in His Word, is what creates community. I must first be diligent to *practice* solitude. I must take time each morning to be alone with God. Then, as I learn through daily discipline to be "alone with God" throughout the day by constantly and consciously setting my eyes on the Lord who is before me, I will develop space in my life that can allow others to share my solitude. In this way community flows out of solitude. The Spirit of God ministers the Word to individual believers and forms them together into a supernatural community as they share their lives together—lives that have been transformed by the Word of God. They then become the Priesthood of Believers.

The Spirit of God gives the Word of God to His Church, the Bride of Christ. We are corporately that Bride. Each of us receives God's special gift of grace as we meditate. We then share not only the love God has given to each of us, but also the knowledge and wisdom that His Spirit imparts to us through His Word. We share our whole lives with one another.

Let us welcome the Holy Spirit, then, as we meditate on God's Word, remembering that the "anointing," that is, the Holy Spirit, abides in us and will interpret and apply God's Word to our lives as we meditate. Let us strive to encourage one another and to build up the Body of Christ worldwide by sharing with other believers the Word that we hear in God's "secret council." (Jeremiah 23:18,19) Then perhaps Jeremiah's great cry will be answered: *"O land, land, land, hear the word of the Lord!"* (Jeremiah 22:29)

A Simple Method for Biblical Meditation

Meditation can best be understood if one actually meditates while reading or studying about meditation. For this reason, we have included Psalm 139 as the meditation application for this book.

As you read this book, then, you will need: your Bible (preferably a completely equivalent translation rather than a paraphrase), a notebook or journal in which you record your insights while meditating, and above all a willingness to set aside fifteen minutes after you read each chapter, to meditate on a verse of Scripture.

King David wrote Psalm 139, and he intended it to be sung.[5] Indeed, this psalm deserves to be sung, over and over. It should be meditated upon and studied with great care. It is a psalm that needs to be memorized and planted in the deep recesses of the mind and heart, for this psalm tells me who I am. It reveals my deepest identity in God. God knows me completely, says the psalmist. He is present with me wherever I go. He is the only source of my life. I am His unique creation, unlike any other, and His thoughts of me would fill more books than ever have been written. His plan for me is perfect, without flaw.

As you meditate on this psalm, you will find yourself beginning to shed whatever doubts you may have harbored about your true identity in Jesus Christ. You will come to know God's love and His care for you in an intimate way. And you will be filled with expectation about His plan for your future.

The message of Psalm 139 has changed peoples' lives throughout the world. I know of a university student who was on the brink of suicide, having lost all hope and meaning of life. Before she made the actual attempt to take her life, she read through this psalm. As she read, she could not take her eyes off of the words "I praise You, for I am fearfully and wonderfully made." She began to experience a strange sensation of being loved and cared for by someone greater than herself. It was at that point that God manifested Himself to her as her Father, the true Source of her life. She continued to read through the psalm, pondering each of the words: " . . . You knitted me together in my mother's womb . . .. I awake, and I am still with You." Then she began to weep quietly before the Lord, committing herself into His loving care and resolving to begin her life anew in Jesus, the Lover of her soul. Today she is a vibrant Christian bearing much fruit for her Lord!

Our method of meditation will be to meditate on one or more verses of this psalm as we complete each chapter of our study. Throughout many centuries of Church history, great numbers of Christians have discovered that meditating verse by verse on a passage of Scripture is the most effective means of meditation. As you read the verse over and over, repeating in your mind these precious words, you will sense that the words of God are beginning to enter your heart and your spirit, not just your mind. And God will meet you through this word. He will speak to you, and your life will be changed, day-by-day. God will reveal Himself to you; and as you enter His presence you will be transformed. Your transformation will not take place instantaneously but will gradually unfold, like a flower that slowly opens to reveal its beauty, until you reflect the glory of the Lord in your own life. Then you will become the "fragrance" of Christ, the "letter" of Christ, to a world that longs to know its Creator.

How then do we meditate? The purpose of this book is to introduce you to biblical meditation and equip you to become a meditator. So let us take a quick glimpse into the basic method of meditation, so you can get started on your journey.

Effective meditation on the Scriptures consists of four steps:

1. Prepare
2. Listen
3. Meet
4. Respond

* Step One—Prepare

Find a comfortable place to sit, remembering that you are the invited guest of Christ Himself, to sit with Him at His banqueting table. Lay aside any hindrances that confuse you as you prepare to enter into sweet fellowship with Him. Confess any known sin. Lay aside heavy burdens or concerns, and prepare to enter His presence.

As you prepare for your meditation, it would be good to read over Psalm 139 and try to understand the meaning of the whole passage. Then, read over the verse on which you will meditate; it would be helpful to read that verse aloud, even fifteen or twenty times.

* Step Two—Listen

Remember that this is God's word *to you, personally.* Your purpose during this time is not to study or merely acquire knowledge or new ideas, but to hear what He has to say to you personally.

Wait upon the Lord. Do not rush through the time, or anxiously try to listen. God is present with you, and His Spirit will speak to you as you simply rest in Him and listen. You may wish to record in your journal what you hear God say to you, or you could write out your prayer to Him. This will help you later, when you want to remember what God has spoken to you.

* Step Three—Meet

When you feel that God has spoken to you, do not stop the meditation time. Rather, take time to seek His face. Ask God to reveal Himself to you in any way He desires. Tell Him that your greatest desire is to see Him and behold the splendor of His face. Open yourself fully to God, and you will meet Him as He opens Himself to you in His Word.

* Step Four—Respond

Meditation is complete only as we respond. The first response is always prayer. Thank God for speaking to you. Pray any other prayer that comes to your mind. Then you will discover that you are beginning to pray the words of the verse on which you have meditated. This becomes a powerful way to pray to God, using His own words of Scripture to pray.

Respond in other creative ways, such as singing a "new song" based on this verse. Paint a picture. Write a poem. Commit yourself to studying this passage more fully. But above all, *obey* all that God says to you through this time of meditation.

As we prepare to meditate on these verses of Psalm 139 we would do well to listen to Henri Nouwen's words about meditation.

As you lie in your bed, drive your car,
        wait for the bus, or walk your dog,
you can slowly let the words [of this verse]
go through your mind simply trying to
listen with your whole being to what they
are saying. You will be constantly distracted
by your worries, but if you keep going back
to the words [of the verse], you will gradually
discover that your worries become less obsessive
and that you really start to enjoy praying.
And as the prayer descends from your mind
into the center of your being
you will discover its healing power[6]

A Note On Bible Translations

Every Bible translator works within the tension of attempting to be literally precise and at the same time striving to produce a readable version. While it is true that no Bible translation is perfect or complete, it is likewise true that the English language possesses many excellent translations.

There are two basic methods of Bible translation: the "word-for-word" approach, which seeks to preserve all the major words of Hebrew and Greek to produce an "essentially literal" translation; and the "thought-for-thought" approach, which sometimes omits certain theological words that would appear to be difficult to the ordinary reader, for the sake of producing readability and "dynamic equivalence."

The best examples of the "thought-for-thought" translations are the NIV (New International Version) and the NJB (New Jerusalem Bible). The classic mainstream of Bible translation has been the "word-for-word" method, typified by the KJV (King James Version), NKJV (New King James Version), the RSV (Revised Standard Version) and the NASB (New American Standard Bible). The most recent version added to this tradition is the ESV (English Standard Version), translated in 2001.

Both methods have their strong and weak points. The "word-for-word" method produces more accurate and clear translations, but the result is often somewhat awkward, with stilted phrases and sentences. The "thought-for-thought" approach produces very readable translations but sometimes at the cost of accuracy and faithfulness to the original text.

The author recommends the use of the ESV (English Standard Version), or other "word-for-word" translations, for study and meditation, particularly when one is meditating word by word through a verse of Scripture. This ESV is highly readable and at the same time accurate and clear.

"I Thank Thee for Thy Word"

My God, I thank Thee for Thy Word
That comes like medicine or a sword,
To change my life that I may be,
In greater likeness unto Thee.

Speak how Thou wilt, that is Thy choice,
In thunder's peal or still small voice,
Thy Word is truth, Thy Word is light
To show me how to live aright.

Reveal Thyself that is my plea
Reveal Thyself O God to me,
Show me Thy will, show me Thy ways,
That I may serve Thee all my days.

"Let there be light," You once did cry,
And brilliant radiance filled the sky,
Command again that light to me,
That I may more Thy glory see.

Thou Living Word, I praise Thy Name
Thou art forevermore the same,
You spoke to prophet, priest and king
Then speak to me, Thy word do bring.

I thirst for Thee My God, My Lord
And open up Thy sacred Word,
I come to drink, I come to feed,
Then meet my very deepest need.

Come, Holy Ghost, come Heavenly Dove,
Show me my Lord, the One I love
And speak to me that I may say,
Yes . . . God spoke to me today.

Give me Lord Thy revelation
Through Thy Word in meditation,
And let it ever to me bring,
The knowledge of my Lord and King.

Campbell McAlpine[7]

Part One

Understanding Meditation

*Meditation becomes as natural as breathing
when we live our lives in the presence
of the One who calls us His friends.
He wants to share with us
all that the Father in His infinite love
has revealed to Him.*

*As I open my Bible
and sit at the feet of Jesus,
the Holy Spirit takes the written Word,
transforms it into a living Word
and plants it in my inner being.*

*I then become
a mobile "Holy of Holies"
whom God will use to
disciple the nations.*

Chapter One

The Meaning of Meditation

A few years before his death at the hands of the German Nazi government, Dietrich Bonhoeffer continued to maintain regular correspondence with men he had once trained in theology, encouraging them to remain steadfast in prayer and meditation. In one letter, written to a soldier on the front lines, he wrote: "Daily, quiet reflection on the Word of God as it applies to me (even if only for a few minutes) becomes for me a point of crystallization for everything which gives interior and exterior order to my life . . .. Meditation is a source of peace, of patience and of joy; it is like a magnet, which draws together all the forces in our life that make for order; it is like deep water which reflects the clouds and the sun on its clear surface. It also serves the Most High by presenting him with a place of discipline, stillness, healing, and contentment in our lives." [1]

Allowing the Holy Spirit to Guide Us

When someone asked him, "What is meditation?" Bonhoeffer replied:

> *Accept the Word of Scripture and ponder it in*
> *your hearts as Mary did. This is all. That is*
> *meditation . . .. We must put ourselves in the*
> *presence of God by slowly, quietly, patiently*
> *advancing from word to word . . . and pause*
> *over each verse while we say it [aloud]. As*
> *the children of Israel journeying through*
> *the wilderness waited for the cloud that was*
> *above the ark to rise and then they were ready*
> *to follow, so we must . . . wait for the Spirit*
> *to guide us. Sometimes He may leave us to*
> *remain silent. At other times He may lead*
> *us onward and open to us trains of spiritual*
> *thought which bring us much joy and strength*
> *in our journey."*[2]

Meditation's very simplicity may mask its transforming power from the casual observer, but for those whose one desire is to dwell in the house of the Lord "to gaze upon the beauty of the Lord and to inquire in his temple," (Psalm 27:4) it holds the secrets both to abundant Christian living and to dynamic ministry in the Holy Spirit.

Mind, Heart and Will

Meditation involves the mind, the heart and the will. We begin by thinking, or reflecting, on the words of Scripture, but we do not want the Word to remain in our minds only. Our desire is that it enter our hearts as well, as we turn our eyes upon Jesus and desire to meet Him in His Word. For some that can become a long journey indeed. But we must make the journey, for the Word of God becomes the Spirit's highway that leads us straight into the presence of God. He does this by causing the Word to deeply penetrate both our minds and our hearts, so that He may redirect our wills to be obedient to the Father.

Meditation Is a Process.

Meditation is not simply a quick action that we do occasionally in order to satisfy our hungry souls. No, it is the process of letting the Word of God come inside and dwell richly in us. "Let the word of Christ dwell in you richly," Paul declares, "teaching and admonishing one another in all wisdom, singing psalms and hymns and spiritual songs, with thankfulness in your hearts to God." (Colossians 3:16)

Meditation is an attitude of turning to the Lord and listening, desiring to hear all He says so that we can obey Him and thereby glorify Him. It is a heart that is so tuned to the Lord that its first desire upon awakening each morning is to hear the Lord speak personally through His Word. Meditation is an attitude of longing for God throughout each day, with the supreme desire of meeting Him and gazing upon His majesty, so that we can walk in intimacy with Him.

Old Testament Teaching On Meditation

The Old Testament words that describe the meditator[3] include the idea of dialogue. Brother Lawrence must have been aware of that when he remarked that the sweetest life is the life lived in continual conversation with God. This lifestyle is both the fruit of meditation and also a good description of the process of meditation. Meditation includes talking to God and listening to what He has to say to us, much as we would do in a human conversation. Meditation will unlock the door to this exciting new life, described by the psalmist in this way: "I have set the Lord always before me; because he is at my right hand, I shall not be shaken." (Psalm 16:8)

Meditation As Worship

The Old Testament Scriptures also speak of meditation as worship. Sometimes the two words—meditation and worship—are used almost synonymously. So we can understand meditation as reading and studying the Scriptures with a heart of worship. Meditation then becomes the foundation of worship. Meditation leads into worship. The true worshiper must first be a true meditator on the Word of God!

The heart of worship is giving, not receiving. We do not worship simply to perform a religious ritual, or to receive a blessing from God. No, we worship the Lord in order to give to Him our deepest love and thanksgiving, as we sing praises to Him. We worship the Lord by presenting our bodies to Him as a living sacrifice, available to be used by Him at any time, in any place, in any way He desires.

Who is blessed more than the worshiper? Who can give testimonies of God's faithfulness and His unfailing provision in every time of need, other than the one who has given everything, including all rights of ownership, to the Lord in wholehearted devotion and worship?

Dear reader, you are worshiping the Lord each time you meditate. Do not seek simply to "get a word for today," or to be rewarded with a life of intimacy with God because of your act of meditation. All that will come, along with much more, as you meditate. But meditate in order to give your whole self to the Lord anew each morning in an act of worship. And you will find, as a meditator, that you cannot outgive God! Meeting God each morning as you meditate on His Word will lead you into a life of deeper worship.

Meditation As Prayer

The Bible also speaks of meditation as prayer. Meditation can be understood as praying the Scriptures in a worshipful attitude. Jesus' disciples asked the Lord to teach them to pray. "Lord, teach us to pray!" Is this not the request that Christians of all ages continue to ask of the Lord? How should we pray? It may sound strange to say that we need to "learn to pray," but we all know that the heart cannot pray by itself. When left to ourselves, we confuse desires, wishes and rejoicings, all of which we can do on our own, without prayer. So we must learn to pray.

How does a child learn to speak? "By listening to the speech of his father," said Dietrich Bonhoeffer. "So we learn to speak to God because God has spoken to us and speaks to us . . .. Repeating God's own words after Him, we begin to pray to Him." He continues, "God's speech in Jesus Christ meets us in the Holy Scriptures. If we wish to pray with confidence and gladness, then the words of Holy Scripture will have to be the solid basis of our prayer . . .. The words which come from God become, then, the steps on which we find our way to God."[4]

As we meditate through the Book of Psalms, especially, we soon find that we are praying the very words of those psalms. The Psalms are the prayer book of the Bible! It is the only book in the Bible that contains mostly prayers! These are the words that Christ Himself prayed centuries ago through King David and the other poets, and He desires to pray those same prayers through us as we meditate. So meditation is the foundation not only of worship but also of prayer.

Meditation, worship and prayer are the heart of the Christian's spirituality. We never concentrate on one at the expense of the others. The intercessor must always be a worshiper and a meditator, or his intercession will simply express human desires. The meditator realizes that the very act of meditation, given to God as an act of worship, leads to even deeper and higher worship, into the very throne room of God the Father, where the true Word is seated at His right hand waiting for all nations to come and worship Him!

New Testament Teaching On Meditation

Both the Old and New Testaments present the same concept of biblical meditation, but some of the emphases are different.[5] The whole Bible speaks of meditation as a process of clearing, or purifying, the mind in order to make room for God and His Word. To meditate is to remove from our minds all things that would obstruct our relationship with God—sins, vain thoughts and imaginations, harboring ill will against others—in order to focus the mind completely on God.

We come to understand meditation more deeply when the Apostle Paul speaks of setting one's mind on things that are above, not things that are below. He speaks of the mind fixed on the Spirit as bringing life, whereas the mind focused on the flesh brings death. He prays that his followers will be filled up with God's Word and even with God Himself. All these are expressions of meditation. The meditating Christian is one who thinks carefully and deeply about his faith. But he goes further and becomes absorbed in the message of salvation in Christ. And the meditator does not stop there, but seeks to fill his thoughts and heart with all that God has said in His Word about Jesus Christ. He fixes his gaze upon Christ and sets his mind on the goal that is before him, of glorifying God through his life and even in death. No wonder, then, that meditators continue to be transformed by the Holy Spirit to make an impact on the world around them!

Three Words to Remember As We Meditate

The biblical teaching on meditation can best be summarized by three words: open, focus, and fill. Remembering these three words as we meditate will enable us to understand the true meaning of biblical meditation, and to learn how to meditate in such a way that we can begin to see dramatic results take place in our lives that will bring blessing to God and to the whole world.

Open

"Open my eyes, that I may behold wondrous things out of your law."[6] So prayed the psalmist. The Holy Spirit must open my spiritual eyes before I can enter into the mysteries of His Word. But does this not indicate that God has first made me blind? God has hidden His Word from mere human analysis and intellectual reasoning. Only the Spirit of God, who is the Author of the Bible, can open my eyes and my mind to grasp the eternal truths of the Word. The greatest Bible scholar would be quick to admit that the deepest realization of the truths of Scripture come not from human endeavor but from revelation by the Spirit of God. The true student of the Bible continually stands in awe as God's Spirit opens his eyes to behold wondrous things that he never could have discovered on his own.

In meditation "a channel is somehow opened between the mind, heart and will—the word the mind receives enters the heart and goes into action via the will."[7] Meditation becomes then a bridge that takes us from knowledge about God to knowledge of God. As we meditate we go beyond truth as we simply perceive it in our minds and begin to search the Scriptures with our whole being, going beyond ideas and concepts to actually experience God!

"Let me remember my song in the night," cried the psalmist. "Let me meditate in my heart. Then my spirit made a diligent search."(Psalm 77:6) Just as God opens His Word to us and opens our eyes to behold His wonders, so also we must open ourselves—spirit, mind, emotions and will—to receive Him. "Behold, I stand at the door and knock," says Jesus. "If anyone hears My voice and opens the door, I will come in to him and eat with him, and he with Me."

(Revelation 3:20) Jesus spoke this word not to unbelievers but to believers, with whom He desired to have deeper intimacy and fellowship. When I open the door not just of my mind but also of my spirit, I "create the emotional and spiritual space which allows Christ to construct an inner sanctuary in my heart."[8] By opening myself to God I am creating space for Him to dwell, a place for Him to deposit His treasures found in each word of His Holy Scripture.

Meditation begins with sitting before a verse of Scripture. "The Lord is my shepherd; I shall not want." Through this one short verse of the twenty-third Psalm, I look to God. I long for His presence. I open myself to God in His Word. I begin to commune with my spirit and not just my mind. I search with my spirit; my spirit ponders as I gaze into the face of my Shepherd. My desire as I meditate is not merely to understand who the Shepherd is, or to make a study of how He provides for me. No, in meditation my great desire is to actually meet the Shepherd, to have a personal encounter and enter into fellowship with Him during this time of meditation. Then surely "I shall not want." How many people's lives have been totally transformed simply by sitting before this one verse of Scripture and allowing the Spirit to meet them and bring them into the presence of the Good Shepherd, who loves His sheep!

Focus

The second key word for meditation is "focus." To meditate is to focus on the words of God which we find in the Scripture text. It is to clear my mind of all unclean or unnecessary thoughts, of all distractions, in order to fix my mind on the Word before me.

The Jewish biblical scholar Aryeh Kaplan[9] reminds us that every person has an "innate capability of remembering everything that has ever happened to him and of perceiving all events that surround him." He remarks that if all this information poured into our minds at once, however, we would be totally overwhelmed and confused. He further points out that the Hebrew word *hitboded,* which means "to be alone," or "to isolate oneself internally," describes meditation as "removing the static" from one's mind—including unnecessary information as well as unhealthy thoughts—in order to allow oneself to focus on the thoughts that God wants to give to us, and upon God Himself.

A good photographer knows that a perfect photograph depends largely on focusing. Proper focusing provides the right light, resulting in the desired result. Meditation is similar. When the meditator focuses on each word of the text, bringing all the powers of his concentration onto the verse, word by word, then his eyes become gradually opened and the hidden treasures revealed.

A Jewish bookstore that I used to frequent in New York City carried many books by Rabbi David Kimchi, one of the most renowned Jewish exegetes and etymologists. He speaks of meditation as "caressing" the subject, removing all other thoughts from the mind in order to concentrate on one idea.[10] It is very much like the new bride who caresses her diamond ring and focuses all her attention on its beauty. She examines it first from one angle, then holds it to the light and closely fixes her attention on another angle. Years later the diamond continues to hold its breathtaking beauty, and one can continue to discover the many facets of its hidden beauty that are revealed to those who will take time to meditate.

The Word of God is like a diamond, a jewel whose beauty still continues to be revealed as the meditator carefully focuses on its meaning, first this facet, then another. No one knows better than the meditator the height of the love of God, the depths of His mercy, the breadth and length of His grace. As the meditator sits before a single verse of Scripture each morning, the Holy Spirit shines the light of the knowledge of the glory of God through each word. The treasure chest of God's Word is opened, and each precious jewel reveals new insights, fresh awareness, and new revelation. Then, we will know that the Lord has spoken indeed.

Meditation is learning to sit with Jesus and learn from Him. Two disciples of Jesus were walking along the road to Emmaus, overwhelmed with a sense of loss over the death of Jesus. He had been their only hope, and now He was gone. Although they did not know it, Jesus had risen from the dead, and now He was walking beside them. Although they did not recognize Him and did not understand (or perhaps could not fully believe) the words He spoke to them as they traveled along, they were captivated by His presence and invited Him into the place where they were staying.

As they were sitting together at table with Jesus, He broke bread with them and continued to share with them all the Scriptures concerning Himself. Luke describes it this way: "When He was at table with them, He took the bread and blessed and broke it and gave it to them."[11] Perhaps these words best describe the process of meditation. Jesus sat at table with them. Most Christians know how to work for Jesus, to run with His vision. Some even know how to walk with Him. But we must learn first of all to sit with Him, totally focused on Him as He speaks the words of His Father to us just as He spoke to Mary of Bethany as she sat at His feet. (Luke 10:38-41)

Is this not meditation? Jesus sits at table with us; He is the host, we the guests. The disciples thought they had invited Jesus when all the while He was the one inviting them. And He invites us each morning to come to His table and sit with Him, focusing all our attention on Him. Jesus then takes the Word, blesses it, breaks it open before us and gives it to us to eat. We simply receive. We meditate by continuing to concentrate on Jesus, focusing on Him alone, listening to everything He wishes to say to us, enjoying His presence, then responding in love, devotion and commitment to that word.

Transformation awaits the believer who will sit with Jesus each morning and meditate on Him and His Word! "And their eyes were opened, and they recognized Him!" Here is the reward to the meditator: We see Jesus! Transformed in His presence, enriched in His Word, we then face each new day with the certainty that He who lives within us will empower us through His Spirit to glorify our Father in heaven!

Fill

The third key word to understand meditation is "fill." Meditation is filling my mind and heart with the Word of God. Our goal as meditators is not to empty ourselves but to be filled with His Word that it may dwell richly within us. Paul actually prays that we "may be filled with all the fullness of God!" (Ephesians 3:19)

To meditate is to hide the Word of God in my heart, daily "filling my treasure chest" with the words that the Spirit speaks to me. The Bible speaks of many people who "hid the Word of God" in their hearts. Joseph's brothers were jealous of his dream and sought to kill him, but his father "kept the saying in mind." Again, Daniel, after having received a vision of the Kingdom of God, said, "I kept the matter in my heart." Centuries later, Mary the mother of Jesus heard the words of the shepherds as they spoke about Jesus. All around her wondered at the words, but Mary "treasured up all these things, pondering them in her heart." (Luke 2:19; see also Genesis 37:11 and Daniel 7:28) The Word stored in the heart produces trust in the One who speaks to us, and obedience to His will.

Meditation is taking a truth we have found, or a mystery we want to understand, and hiding it in the depths of our hearts, believing that the Holy Spirit will reveal its meaning and power to our inner spirits.

Nearly three decades have passed since I first learned meditation from Campbell McAlpine, one of the great Bible meditators and perhaps the best teacher on the subject. He describes meditation as "the devotional practice of pondering the words of a verse, or verses, of Scripture with a receptive heart, allowing the Holy Spirit to take the written Word and apply it as the living Word to the inner being."[12] I remember sitting at his feet (actually standing beside him and interpreting while he spoke on Bible meditation to great crowds of eager listeners in Korea) and marveling at how the Holy Spirit, the Author of the Scriptures, transforms the written Word into the living Word and then plants it in my innermost being, so that the seed of the Word begins to take root and blossom in my life, producing fruit for the Lord. He goes on to say that meditation "is the practice of pondering, considering, and reflecting on verses of Scripture in total dependence on the Holy Spirit to give revelation of truth and meaning, and by obedient response and reception of that Word, having it imparted to the inner being . . .. Meditation is inwardly receiving truth."[13]

One of the meanings of the word "meditation" is "to chew the cud." God created the bovine animals, such as the deer, the cow or sheep, with loving care. He gave them four stomachs so that they could eat quickly in the open field and then "chew the cud" under the protection of trees in the forest, away from predatory animals. The deer or cow will eat large amounts of food quickly, and then swallow the food. It goes into its first stomach only to be regurgitated after fifteen or twenty seconds. The animal then slowly chews the food before swallowing it into his second stomach, and again regurgitates it. This action is repeated until the food reaches the fourth stomach, at which time it is perfectly digested. A veterinarian friend of mine remarked that these animals will often chew the cud up to eight or twelve hours! And this is what it means to meditate! To chew the cud!

A group of Sri Lankan pastors had gathered for a seminar on spirituality at a small deer farm and youth rehabilitation center near Colombo, the capitol. They seemed unable to grasp the meaning of meditation, until we all went outside to observe the deer as they "meditated," or chewed the cud. After about thirty minutes of observation, one of the pastors remarked, "Ah, now I understand! To meditate is to slowly chew the Word of God, not looking for some new idea or a sermon to preach, just slowly and patiently digesting the Word that God gives me!" Indeed this is the secret of meditation—to slowly ponder each word of the verse, not seeking new knowledge or materials to use for some other purpose but rather to receive all that God's Spirit desires to feed me. The Spirit of Jesus is the initiator in meditation; I am the recipient. My only desire is to eat what He feeds me, to rest in the word that He wants to give me each day, to ruminate on the word, tasting it and enjoying it, always listening to what God wants to say to me personally each day.

"Your words were found, and I ate them, and your words became to me a joy and the delight of my heart, for I am called by Your name, O Lord, God of hosts." (Jeremiah 15:16) So spoke Jeremiah. He was a meditator, inwardly receiving the Word of God. Jesus Himself spoke to His disciples, saying, "It is the Spirit who gives life; the flesh is of no avail. The words that I have spoken to you are spirit and life.' (John 6:63)

Here is the secret of growth: God's words are living words, and the more we allow the Word of God to fill us, the greater the power of God's Spirit, the Anointing who dwells within us. And the more abundant is the life of Christ in us. We simply have to feast on the Word of God each day, allowing God to feed us and fill us with that Word. I remember Campbell McAlpine once remarked concerning

God's provision of manna to the Israelites in the wilderness: "Here was 'bread from heaven' to feed and sustain them. What did the people do when they saw it? Admire it, analyze it, or dissect it? No. They ate it, inwardly received it." This is what happens in meditation. We eat the Word; we are filled with it, and our souls are satisfied with the presence of the Lord.

Meditation, Study and Contemplation

Certainly meditation is one of the most effective ways of getting to know God through His Word, but it is not the only way. The believer must also read the Word, study it, listen to it, memorize it, sing it and proclaim it. In particular, we must distinguish between meditation and study, and between meditation and contemplation. In doing so we will come to understand more deeply the meaning and value of meditation in the Christian life.

Meditation and Study

To ask God to open my eyes that I may discover wondrous things in His Word is the beginning of both Bible study and Bible meditation. Both are important. Study and meditation go hand in hand. "Meditation, as it were, sits on the shoulders of faithful and reverent Bible study."[14]

We study the Bible in order to understand and grasp the truths of Scripture with our minds so that we may know God, obey His truth and teach it to others. Bible research and study done faithfully and reverently by professors and teachers of the Faith will provide a rich background for the ordinary believer to understand and appropriate the truths of the Christian Faith. How thankful we must be for scholars who dedicate their entire lives to translating the Scriptures, to performing faithful biblical exegesis and interpretation, to writing commentaries and compiling concordances, Bible dictionaries and background studies that will enable the believer to understand the Bible! Ordinary Christians also must study the Bible, using the many tools that are readily available. In addition, every Christian can study the Bible inductively[15] and discover the depths of the Word.

But at some point in his study, the truly great Bible scholar will discover that he is "falling in love with the Word of God." It becomes more than the pursuit of academic knowledge. He becomes captivated by the Word, possessed by its magnetic power that comes from the Spirit. Many scholars testify to the way their study of the Bible flows naturally into meditation. Rather than being a barrier, consecrated study actually leads into meditation on the Scriptures. Although Bible study and Bible meditation have different functions, neither one is possible without the other. God illumines our minds in order that we may see the message that He has for each one of us and meet Him in His Word.

Peter Toon offers three analogies, which serve to highlight the way the Bible is the source of meditation by the Church. First, meditation can be seen as disciples reading their most highly respected teacher's writing. A disciple would carefully and devotedly read every word of his teacher, often taking time to ponder even one word, searching for suggested meanings or indirect meanings that would not be observed by a casual reader. Second, the meditator can be seen as a soldier reading his orders before battle. The soldier could not afford to miss even a single word of his orders. He would read them so many times that he would memorize them without even realizing that he was doing so. His orders for battle would become imprinted on his mind, and he would ponder them and repeat them to himself as he prepared for battle.

But his third analogy is the most powerful. He describes the Scriptures as being like a long love letter sent from heaven by the Bridegroom, Jesus Christ, to His Bride, the

Church.[16] The Bride savors the letter with tenderness and with great expectancy. She will discover hidden treasures in the letter that a mere Bible interpreter could never see. She is a meditator, sitting at the feet of Jesus, her Lover, to love and worship Him by hearing and responding to His unique message of love that is for her alone.

These analogies point to the inseparable relationship between study of the Word of God and meditating on that Word. Biblical knowledge enables the meditator to better understand the things that he experiences as God meets him and speaks directly to him in his times of meditation.

Jesus met Saul on the Damascus road and spoke great mysteries to him, opening up to him the rich treasures of all the words that had been spoken about the Christ. Paul as a scholar spent his entire life seeking to understand the mysteries of the Incarnation, and his writings reveal also the depth of his meditation on the Incarnation, the Cross, the love of God, and all the wealth of treasures available to each Christian.

Perhaps Saint Francis had the correct approach to the Word of God. This is how John Michael Talbot describes him:

> *Saint Francis was not a professional scholar of the Bible, but unwearied application to prayer and the continual practice of virtue had purified his spiritual vision, so that his keen intellect was bathed in the radiance of eternal light and penetrated its depths. Free from every stain, his genius pierced to the heart of its mysteries, and by effective love he entered where theologians [of his day] and their science stood outside. Once he had read something in the sacred book and understood its meaning, he impressed it indelibly on his*

memory; anything that he had once grasped carefully, he meditated upon continuously. This is why theologians of his era said of him, "His theology soars aloft on the wings of purity and contemplation, like an eagle in full flight, while our learning crawls along on the ground!"[17]

Meditation and Contemplation

Just as meditation and study have different functions yet compliment each other, so also do meditation and contemplation. Contemplation flows out of meditation. Or we could say that at some point our meditation on the Scriptures leads us into contemplation of God. There is much excitement today among many Christians who seem to have "discovered" contemplation. I applaud the movement toward contemplative prayer, but not because it is a new trend in the Church (it has been around since the days of the Early Church), and not because it is something separate from meditation on the Scriptures. Meditation and contemplation cannot be separated but always must exist together.

Since the early centuries of Christianity, contemplation has been understood to be an "experience of God." We seek God in order to meet Him and love Him more devotedly, so that we can serve Him without hesitation or reservation. But we always begin with meditation on the Word of God. We cannot "skip the Word" and go directly into "higher prayer" that excludes the Word of God. Only the believer who has laid in his life a foundation of meditating on the Word of God, continually listening to hear what God would say to him each new day, only such a believer is able to take the next step of meeting God face to face and gazing upon His beauty and majesty. Christian spirituality never exists without, or goes beyond, the Word of God.

When then does "meditation" become "contemplation?" Again, we must be careful about engaging in what could be abstract discussion of spiritual matters. Even though such discussion is popular today, it was not so among our forbearers of the faith. Thomas Merton sums it up well when he says, "The only way in which we can at last enter into the possession of these realities . . . is to stop talking about them and lay hands on them by living them out" as we seek to know and love God more. If we meditate faithfully on the Bible, God will manifest Himself to us. We meet Him and that is contemplation."[18]

Merton speaks of liturgical prayer in much the same way we would speak of meditation, and he states that meditation turns into contemplation "as soon as our prayer [meditation] ceases to be a search for God and turns into a celebration, by interior experience, of the fact that we have found Him!"[19] Is this not what the disciples experienced on the road to Emmaus, when they heard Jesus speak, listening intently to His words as He broke bread with them, and then suddenly "their eyes were opened and they recognized Him?" (Luke 24:30-31)

Meditation is not contemplation; rather it leads to contemplation. But the same Holy Spirit inspires Christians to be engaged in both. It is He who inspired the Scriptures and who opens to us deeper meanings of the words on which we meditate. And through that same Word, He leads us beyond the "word" of the Scriptures to the true Word, Jesus Christ. Beyond all the words of Scripture lies the Word who is the Way, the Truth and the Life. We are delighted when we hear Him speak, but our delight becomes ecstasy when we behold Him who is speaking. When the Emmaus Road disciples heard Jesus speak, their hearts were burning within them. But when they actually beheld Him, they were filled with unspeakable joy that had to be shared. This is because "the heart of meditation is the sheer enjoyment of the pres-

ence of the living God and the delight that comes in praising
His name."[20] All these treasures await us as we begin our
journey into meditation on the Word of God and contemplation of His presence.

Invitation to the Banquet Table
Personal Meditation on Psalm 139

1. Review the four simple steps of meditation:
First, prepare your heart.
Second, listen to all God wants to say to you through the
text.
Third, seek to meet God as He reveals Himself to you.
Fourth, respond to Him in prayer and obedience.

2. Read through Psalm 139 in its entirety.
Open yourself to God and listen as you read.
Try to understand what the psalmist wants to express
through this psalm.

3. Meditate on Psalm 139, **verse 1.**
Oh Lord, you have searched me and known me!
Consider that God knows everything about you and that He
searches your heart.
He searches not to judge you but to love you more
completely.
Ask Him what He knows about your inmost being.
Listen to what the Lord wants to say to you personally!

4. Write down in your Meditation Journal what the Lord
says to you.
Or you may write out your prayer to Him.
Allow the Spirit to lead you as you listen to the Lord.

5. Take time now to *wait upon the Lord.*
Give Him your heart. Ask Him to reveal Himself to you.

6. Spend time in prayer.
Thank God for His word to you.
Commit yourself to obeying Him.

Chapter Two

Seven Keys To Becoming A Meditator

S ome years ago two friends, at different times and places, placed two books in my hands, which greatly altered the way I approach the Scriptures and prayer. One book, entitled *Prayer,* by Hans Urs von Balthasar,[1] was published originally in German under the title *Das Betrachtende Gebet,* in 1955. But it was not until more than thirty years later that the book appeared in English. The author emphasizes the power of the Word of God not only in communicating knowledge about God, but also in leading the reader to meet God personally and be transformed through His Word. Rather than the Bible's being a book that we can easily master, God Himself appears through the pages of His book, and the book masters the reader! In von Balthasar's words, "God's epiphany compels the hearer to kneel in humble submission."[2]

The other book is *Opening to God: A Guide to Prayer,* by Thomas H. Green, S.J.[3] The author speaks of meditation as being the foundation for prayer. As we listen to God each day in His Word and seek to obey Him, we learn to listen to Him throughout the day. He defines prayer as an opening of the mind and heart toward God, which leads us to encounter Him in love. This love relationship with God, through listening to Him, becomes the foundation for prayer. These two books would be of great benefit to anyone who seeks to become a meditator on the Word of God or an intercessor led by the Spirit to pray the prayers of God.

The following "keys" to becoming a meditator do not all originate with the authors of these two books. On the contrary, God has revealed many of them to me over the course of the many years that I have been a meditator. Still, I am deeply grateful to the authors of these books, and to my friends who surprised me by giving them to me. Both books have helped me understand more clearly the heart of a meditator. Here, then, are some keys to becoming an effective Bible meditator.

1. We are born to be meditators.

We are born to meditate, created to hear and respond to God's Word. God placed the mystery of Himself deep within us, and our hearts will never be content until we meet this God personally through His Word. St. Augustine must have been thinking of this when he said, in his *Confessions,* that God created us for Himself and our hearts would never find true rest until they find that rest in Him. God created us with imagination and desire to seek Him and the capacity to hear Him when He speaks. Von Balthasar puts it this way: "Man was created to be a hearer of the word, and it is in responding to the word that he attains his true dignity."[4]

The Bible is not a scholars' book, inaccessible to the average reader. No, the Holy Spirit enables every Christian to hear God as He speaks through His Word. This does not mean that we no longer need to study, or that the Church needs no biblical scholars. On the contrary, there is a great urgency today for young men and women who will commit themselves to a lifelong pursuit of consecrated Bible study. The greater our understanding of the mysteries of God's

Word, the more depth we find in meditation. But it must be stated emphatically that we need no special training to hear God speak, no advanced degrees, no special position in the Church. God will meet us where we are. He will speak to us, and we can hear Him when He speaks. There is no formula, only a relationship.

God provided the Tabernacle for Moses and the people of Israel as they traveled through the wilderness. Deep inside was the "Holy of Holies," where the high priest met God. Moses likewise would go daily into the "Tent of Meeting," and there God would speak to him face to face, as a man speaks to his friend. (Exodus 33:9-11) Where is the "Holy of Holies" today, the "Tent of Meeting?" It is inside us, where the Triune God dwells, Father, Son and Holy Spirit! We do not have to search far and wide to hear God speak, nor do we need to erect an edifice where we must go to meet Him. His Spirit is within us. He speaks to us daily. We just have to "dust off" our inner sanctuary, and prepare to listen. The greatest thing we can do is to make room in our hearts for God's Word to dwell. *I am* a meditator. *You are* a meditator. We must listen to *Him!*

2. We must meditate on the Bible, not some book about the Bible.

"We take up a book of 'meditations' which presents us, ready-made, with the contemplation we ought to produce for ourselves," declares von Balthasar.[5] He maintains that when we use another person's meditations, we are simply observing someone else eating, but it does nothing to fill our stomachs. The person who wrote the material for our "quiet time," or for our "morning watch," obviously feasted well on God's Word. But what do we feast on? Another person's interpretation of that Word. That is not meditation.

The small books that many of us use for our devotional times can be very helpful. We appreciate their insights, enjoy their illustrations, and even engage in constructive Bible study through their questions and guidelines. And Christians do grow through using such materials. But we actually are doing "spiritual reading," not meditating. Perhaps we would do better to spend this time reading the great Christian classics, even a page or a small section each day, rather than most contemporary devotional booklets. We could then grow with the saints: with Brother Lawrence through his book *Practicing the Presence of God;* or with Hannah Whitehall Smith through her book *The Christian's Secret of a Happy Life*. And, of course, there are countless others we could mention.

The Christian must learn to meet God and hear His voice directly through His Word, meditating directly on the *Bible* and not some book that explains the Bible. To meditate, we need no commentary, no devotional booklet, no stories or illustrations, no questions for which we must write out answers. No, we simply need the Bible! For that is where we meet God, and where we hear Him speak.

3. God Himself is the subject of all meditation.

When we meditate on the pages of Scripture, we actually are meditating on *God Himself* who reveals Himself through the words. We are meditating on God, not on the printed page. Likewise when we meditate on a beautiful sunset, or on a majestic mountain peak, we are in reality meditating on the greatness of God who created nature so that we might meet Him through its grandeur. God Himself is the subject of the Christian's meditation. Whether we meditate on His words, His works of salvation, His wonders of creation, or on the good, upright and honorable things He allows us to see, we *always are meditating on God Himself.* These things are vehicles through which God reveals Himself to us.

Meditation is a tool given by God to help the Christian grow. Just as a tool itself cannot build a house, but can do so only when placed in the hands of a master carpenter, so also meditation, practiced by the believer who places himself in God's hands and relies totally on the Holy Spirit, will bring life-changing blessings. Meditation in itself will not help us, but *Jesus* will pour out the blessings of His Father on us when we meditate!

4. We must remember who we are as we meditate.

We meditate effectively only when we approach God's Word with confidence as to our true identity. And who are we? "We are His workmanship, created in Christ Jesus for good works," proclaims the Apostle Paul. (Ephesians 2:10) Another translation would be, "We are His *work of art,*" or "God's *poem!*"[6] Indeed we are His children, adopted into His family through the sacrifice of His Son Jesus Christ on the Cross of Calvary. We are God's sons and daughters!

When we come into the place of meditation, then, we come not as beggars but rather as His children whom He *always* invites to come boldly into His presence. We do not need to "work ourselves up" to become more spiritual before we meditate. We already are spiritual; we are complete in Him. Our righteousness is the righteousness of Christ, so we need not be concerned about our unworthiness or lack of qualification to enter His throne room. Neither do we need to search for a certain mood or atmosphere that makes us feel "ready" to meditate. We simply come to him as a child, running into the arms of a waiting Father. When the prodigal son returned home, he had practiced what he would say, and how he would act, when he first met his father. But the father allowed him no room for self-criticism or feelings of unworthiness. Instead his father ran to him and took him into his arms, and bestowed on him all his once lost blessings of sonship.

This is how we should approach our Father when we come to meditate on His Word. Meditating on the Word of God is like coming to a great feast. God Himself has prepared it for us, and we must come as invited guests each morning and not as beggars who really do not expect to receive much. Someone has said that meditation must be done from a New Testament position, as Christians redeemed by the blood of the Lamb through the grace of God, not as Old Covenant believers who still need to justify themselves by works of the law in order to enter God's presence. The walls of separation have been broken down; the Holy of Holies is now open, the curtain that once separated us from God now rent asunder. Once again we can see that basic Bible knowledge is impor-tant for one who wishes to be a meditator—knowledge of His great work for us and of who we are in Him.

5. We do not meditate to get something from God.

For many years during my early ministry I found it diffi-cult to approach the Bible and hear God speak to me directly. One of the chief reasons was that I was meditating in order to get something specific from God: an answer to a prayer, a word to pass on, or ideas for a sermon to preach. My breakthrough in meditation came only as I realized that the purpose of meditation is to wait upon God. The meditator's posture is one of waiting, not working, not running. But it is not waiting for some *thing* but rather for *Someone!* We meditate not to get something we want from God, but rather to *meet* God daily, to come into His presence with a spirit of worship, seeking to gaze into His wondrous face and behold His beauty and then to *listen to whatever He wants to say* to us. I have come to understand that we pastors and teachers of the Word of God may have an even more difficult time listening to God than does the average Christian who simply wants to know God!

To meditate is not to seek an answer to a specific prayer, nor to get material for the next week's sermon. Yet the pastor who dwells abundantly in the Word of God through daily meditation will never lack a sermon to preach. To meditate is not to attempt to receive some "great word" from the Lord. No, it is to embrace, with my whole mind, heart and will, whatever Word He gives me, even if it is simply a brief word such as "Follow Me," and to commit myself to trust Him through that Word and follow Him unreservedly.

Meditation has no human agenda. It is rather a prayer of committal: "Lord, whatever You desire to show me, *that alone* is what I want from You!" As we come to Him daily with this attitude, surely the gates of heaven will be opened to us and we will receive guidance from the Lord even before we ask Him, and blessings we have not even sought. We will become *saturated* with God's Word. Just as a sponge becomes saturated with water, so our desire as Christians is to be so filled with the Word of God that we are always ready to do His will. We become like the root of a tree drawing sustenance from the soil and the water—a living, organic relationship—that places us in the "ready" position, available for God. This is the power of meditation.

6. We should expect to be transformed as we meditate.

To meditate is to meet God. We look to Him through His Word, with hearts of love and reflection, with the desire to hear all He wants to say to us so that we might obey His will. A. W. Tozer once said that faith is simply gazing into the face of God, laying down our problems and impossibilities and fixing our eyes upon Him who is the answer to all our deepest needs and desires.

But there is an even greater truth. *God Himself* is also gazing at me as I meditate! A secret of effective meditation, then, is to approach the Word of God with the realization that He desires to meet me even more than I desire to meet Him! We often think we must invite God to come into our presence, but actually He is the one who invites us. The disciples on the road to Emmaus invited Jesus to come into their dwelling and have a meal with them, only to discover that Jesus Himself was inviting them! And so it is with meditation.

God is looking at us when we meditate. He who sees all and knows all now sees us, not as sinners unworthy to come before Him, but as His precious children who desire to know Him and to walk more intimately with Him. He does not fix His gaze upon our weaknesses but upon the longings of our hearts. When Jesus called Simon Peter to be His disciple, He told him that He would no longer call him "Simon," which means "reed," like a plant in water, unstable, easily broken, having no foundation; rather He would call him "Peter," which means rock, one with a strong foundation. That is how He saw Peter and that is how He sees us as we come to Him.

What happens then, as God casts His loving gaze upon us and we fix our eyes upon His beauty and holiness? We are *transformed!* We are transformed daily as we meditate upon God and His Word. As we meditate we are not looking to ourselves, not searching our inner beings for meaning and reality. We are not looking for principles to apply. No, we are looking to God! And He is looking to us! And we are changed. Transformation does not come by listening to a famous preacher deliver a sermon, or by attending a seminar. No, transformation comes in the hour of solitude, when we are alone with our Master who delights to see us in His presence. Remember this as a secret for growth: we *always* will be transformed when we meditate on the Word of God, not because we are seeking something for ourselves, but because we go beyond ourselves and meet God.

7. Meditation prepares us to be God's instruments in world evangelization.

We are renewed personally when we meditate. We explore the mystery of God Himself—Father, Son and Holy Spirit—and enter into new intimacy with Him and are transformed in our whole being. Yet we must never forget that the mystery of the Gospel of Jesus Christ is for *all humankind!* True meditation always drives us outward into the world, not inward to our own selves. God meets us personally as we meditate; He gives us a word that is for us personally, before He gives us a word to preach or teach. He seeks to transform us through times of solitude, alone with Him.

But He transforms us through His Spirit not for the purpose of making us more spiritual Christians, separated from the world to enjoy His presence alone. He gives to us that we may give to the world. He blesses us, that we may become His source of blessing for others, and for the nations, just as He promised Abraham. The meditating Christian is the "world Christian," embracing God's heart for a lost and suffering world.

We are called to share the truth of the Gospel to the world. But that truth can be shared only as it becomes our own personal truth, applied first to our own lives. Then as we become transformed and the truth begins to set us free, we become God's instruments to transform the world.

Words of Caution and Encouragement

It would be good here to give some words of caution but also of encouragement. First, a word of caution: A Christian should be careful about engaging in meditation that is not

Christian meditation, whether it be yoga as a spiritual discipline, transcendental meditation, or meditation as practiced by other religions. The basic difference between Christian and non-Christian meditation is that non-Christian forms of meditation have no object other than the meditator himself or a principle or an idea. There is no subject of their meditation that can reveal itself to the meditator. Christian meditation, on the other hand, always has a subject. That subject is the living God who manifests Himself, who speaks and enters into dialogue with me, and who transforms me as I enter His presence. Meditators in other religions are searching for their "true self," while Christian meditators are searching for their "true Maker," the God and Father of our Lord Jesus Christ.[7]

Thomas Merton gives a penetrating comparison between Christian and non-Christian meditation. He speaks of Creation as having been given to man as a "clean window through which the light of God could shine into men's souls."[8] But after the fall and the resulting degradation, the nations, or people groups, were no longer able to understand the world they lived in. Rather than seeing the sun as a witness to God, they began to worship the sun itself as a god. The ensuing darkness that settled upon their universe caused them to be afraid of the sun, of trees, or of the stars. All these beautiful things which God gave to us and which witness to God became for them rather objects that had to be placated.

Using a windowpane to symbolize this, he compares this corruption with what happens to a window when a room no longer receives light from the outside. During the daylight hours we can see though the window. When night comes, we can still see through it, if there is no light inside our room. But when we turn the lights on, we can only see ourselves reflected in the windowpane. The problem is that the nations that did not know God began to light lamps of their own, since they could not see God's light. And they thought this reflection they saw in the windowpanes was another spiritual world. Some of the greater religious leaders, notably Buddha, had more insight. But his insight was also limited. Merton says that "Buddha knew too well that the reflections in the window were only projections of our own existence and our own desires, but did not know that this was a window, and that there could be sunlight outside the glass!"[9]

But here are some words of encouragement: First, we must recognize that although some forms of non-Christian meditation are demonic and destructive, still other forms of meditation, found in the major religions of the world, are an expression of those people's search for God. Not able to find Him, still they are longing to know Him and are diligently searching for the source of meaning in their lives. We should view such people not with a judgmental spirit but with compassion, and pray that, as they travel along as pilgrims, they might meet the One who seeks to reveal Himself to them.

Second, a word of personal encouragement to you, dear reader. As you begin, or continue, your pilgrimage into the Word of God as a meditator, ask God to reveal to you the truth that you indeed *are a* meditator, that you can hear Him as He speaks to you daily. Spend time in His Word, become a man or woman of the Word, ready to obey all that God speaks to you to do. Expect to be renewed daily as you meditate, knowing that He Himself will bear His fruit through your life, that you may glorify Him all your days.

two kinds of meditators

1) Non Christian

2) Christian

Invitation to the Banquet Table
Personal Meditation on Psalm 139

1. Review the four simple steps of meditation:
First, prepare your heart.
Second, listen to all God wants to say to you through the text.
Third, seek to meet God as He reveals Himself to you.
Fourth, respond to Him in prayer and obedience.

2. Read through the entire chapter of Psalm 139.
Open yourself to God and listen as you read.
Try to understand what the psalmist wants to express through this psalm.

3. Meditate on Psalm 139, **verse 2.**
You know when I sit down and when I rise up;
You discern my thoughts from afar.
Remember that God's eye is upon you to bless you as you rise each morning.
He knows your thoughts. He wants to share His thoughts with you.
Listen to what the Lord wants to say to you personally!

4. Write down in your Meditation Journal what the Lord
says to you.
Or you may write out your prayer to Him.
Allow the Spirit to lead you as you listen to the Lord.

5. Take time now to *wait upon the Lord.*
Give Him your heart. Ask Him to reveal Himself to you.

6. Spend time in prayer,
Thank God for His word to you.
Commit yourself to obey Him.

Chapter Three

Solitude, Silence and the Word

Solitude As a Lifestyle

Enoch was one of the greatest meditators who ever lived. His life was consumed by God. He found no meaning apart from God, no joy that arose from any source other than God, no sorrows that he could not share with God. He searched for God with his spirit and focused his entire life on God. He allowed the Holy Spirit to fill him completely with God Himself. The writer of *Genesis* puts it simply, *"Enoch walked with God, and he was not, for God took him."*[1] Before Enoch was taken up to God, the author of Hebrews adds, he was commended as having pleased God by his faith. (Hebrews 11:5)

Is this not the essence of the spiritual life—simply to walk with the Lord, led and empowered by His Spirit? Andrew Murray wrote that our goal should be to walk so closely with the Lord that we can hear Him even when He whispers to us, and to walk so devotedly before Him that we are always ready to do His will.

The psalmist would say it this way: "I have set the Lord always before me; because he is at my right hand, I shall not be shaken." (Psalm 16:8) To consciously seek to be in the presence of the Lord, to confess that I desire to be with Him, just as He desires to be with me, is the beginning of our spiritual journey. Jesus chose His twelve disciples first of all "to be with Him,'" to enter into fellowship with Him so that He could share the treasures of His Father with them. Then, and only then, did He send them out to proclaim the Gospel and give them power to cast out demons. (Mark 3:13-15)

This is the life of solitude. Wherever we are, whatever we do, we live our lives in the presence of the One who knows and loves us completely, with the one goal of pleasing Him. Solitude is to be "alone with God," even in the midst of a great crowd. When our ministry's office was located in New York City, I would often stroll the busy, noisy sidewalks of Manhattan's Time Square. I wondered if it were possible to be alone with God in the midst of all the bright lights and deafening noises of the city. God assured me that I was in His presence there, just as surely as if I had been in a prayer chapel in a quiet country village. Christ is present with us always. When I turn to see the One who is always before me, I am filled with His presence. Our entire ministry flows out of this dwelling in the gentle, healing presence of Christ, our Savior and Lord.

Meditation becomes as natural as breathing, when we live our lives in the presence of the One who calls us His friends, and who wants to share with us all that the Father in His infinite love has revealed to Him. (John 15:15) A meditator is not a saint who must separate himself from the world, protected from the affairs of daily life so as not to lose his spirituality. No, a meditator is a saint who walks with Christ into the marketplace, who communes with Him while doing the morning dishes, or while managing a large engineering project. A meditator is one who walks in solitude, always listening, always ready to obey.

Solitude As a Daily Discipline

To achieve this goal of walking with the Lord, of "practicing the presence of God," as Brother Lawrence would say, we must begin by setting aside a special time of solitude each day—a time to be alone with God. This is the time each day when we finally can begin to let go of our compulsions and fears, our lusts and anger, and enter into the gentle, healing presence of Jesus.

Henri Nouwen speaks of this time alone with God as a time of emptying and a time of filling.[2] It is a time to daily relinquish my rights, to give up my "false self" by facing myself as I actually am. He speaks of the twins that make up my false self: greed and anger. Greed is my basic self-centeredness; anger my impulsive response of being deprived, or of feeling unjustly treated.[3] This is the time, perhaps the only time of the day, when in the presence of my loving Father I confront myself as I am with all my evil thoughts, bad habits, compulsive behavior and rebellion.

A Time of Struggle. Daily solitude is often a time of struggle, a time where I have to deal with my negative thoughts, my pride and stubbornness. I am struggling not just against Satan or the world, but I am struggling also with myself. But as I do so in the presence of the Lord, standing in His grace, I am doing so in the power of His Holy Spirit who desires to make me whole.

Nouwen speaks of this time of daily solitude as a "hot furnace," or as the "crucible of transformation."[4] Perhaps it is very much like the fiery furnace in which Daniel's three friends were freed from the cords that bound them. This is a time of repentance, a time to be set free from the sin and habits that cling so closely. Most of us would prefer our morning quiet time with the Lord to be peaceful and filled with joy. Indeed God does want us to enjoy great peace of soul and joy. But sometimes His Spirit needs to stir our spirits first, so that we can empty ourselves of our negative thoughts and sins.

A Time of Meeting. The Holy Spirit wants to make our daily solitude a time of encounter with the Lord, and not just a time of inner struggle. As we empty ourselves before the Lord, we desire then to be filled by Him. We want to be filled with His love that takes away our fears. Our desire is to *meet* Him. As I lay aside my rights and lay down my greed and anger, I then invite Jesus to enter into all the areas of my life. Each morning becomes a time of encounter with Jesus, a time of dwelling in His love, of receiving His healing for my tired spirit.

Andrew Murray describes this daily abiding in the presence of the Lord, the "most holy place," in the following way:

> *Oh the blessedness of a life in the Holiest! Here the Father's face is seen and His love tasted. Here His holiness is revealed and the soul made partaker of it. Here the sacrifice of love and worship and adoration, the incense of prayer and supplication, is offered in power. Here the outpouring of the Spirit is known as an ever-streaming, overflowing river, from under the throne of God and the Lamb. Here the soul, in God's presence, grows into more complete oneness with Christ, and more entire conformity to His likeness . . . Here the soul mounts up as on eagle's wings, the strength is renewed, and the blessing and the power*

and the love are imparted with which God's priests can go out to bless a dying world. Here each day we may experience the fresh anointing, in virtue of which we can go out to be the bearers, and witnesses, and channels of God's salvation to men, the living instruments through whom our blessed King works out His full and final triumph! O Jesus! Our great High Priest, let this be our life![5]

Silence and Meditation

Silence is the home of the Word. T.S. Eliot, in his poem *"Ash Wednesday,"* lamented, "Where shall the word be found, where will the word resound? Not here, there is not enough silence." Only as we wait in silence before the Lord can we hear Him speak. It was essential for Elijah to hear the Lord speak to him as he was fleeing from Jezebel. The word of the Lord came to him while he was taking refuge in a cave at Mount Horeb. But it did not come the way Elijah expected, not in the strong wind or the mighty earthquake, neither in the fire. Instead, the voice of the Lord came to Elijah in the sound of a low whisper. One translation says "in the sound of sheer silence."

Biblical silence is not the absence of words. It is not to sit passively and wait for something to happen. Rather, silence is an attitude, or posture, of turning one's ear to listen. When we are silent before the Lord, waiting upon Him in His Word, or being attentive to Him throughout the day as we do our daily chores, He will speak.

Yet many people are afraid of silence; for them it is threatening. Formerly we had a youth ministry in New York City, ministering to young junior and senior high school students. The youth pastors in the city discovered that a key problem with the youth was that they were "meditating" on the wrong things. They were focusing their minds and filling their thoughts and emotions with destructive music and violent video games. So we would take them to summer camp and teach them to meditate on the Word of God. We would instruct the young people to take their Bibles and go sit under a tree for fifteen minutes and ask God to speak to them. We allowed no CD players, no tape recorders, no internet connection. "Just be silent before the Lord and wait for Him to speak," we told them.

One young student lasted only three minutes! He rushed back into camp complaining, "It's so noisy, I can't stand the noise!" But there were no noises in the Pocono Mountains where we held camp, only the sounds of a gently flowing stream or of birds singing. "No, it's so noisy *inside* me!" he cried, "I don't know what to do!" It was at this point that we realized that there are actually two kinds of silence: a frightening, fearful silence and a peaceful silence.

We took the outside noises away, but the young student did not experience inner silence. On the contrary, the noise *inside* him became noisier than the noise outside! His anger, and his many fears began shouting at him, so much so that he said he could not stand the silence.

Many people seek to meditate on the Word of God, to have a Quiet Time when they can leave the noise and bustle of everyday life and be silent before the Lord. Yet they discover that the noise is actually inside them, not outside. And they are left unsatisfied. But a key to becoming an effective meditator is to learn that we do not go *inside* ourselves to find peace and quiet. No, we must go *beyond* ourselves, into the presence of God, to find the peaceful silence that allows us to hear His Word.

The following is a tale from the Desert Fathers during the early centuries of the Christian Church. A young disciple asked his teacher how to find silence.

"Would you teach me silence?" I asked.
"Ah!" He seemed to be pleased. "Is it the Great Silence
that you want?" "Yes, the Great Silence."
"Well, where do you think it is to be found?" he asked.
"Deep within me, I suppose. If only I could go deep
within, I'm sure I'd escape the noise at last. But it's
hard.
Will you help me?" I knew he would. I could feel his
concern, and his spirit was so silent.
"Well, I've been there," he answered. "I spent years
going in. I did taste the silence there. But one day Jesus
came—maybe it was my imagination—and said simply,
'Come, follow me.' I went out, and I've never gone
back."
I was stunned. "But the silence . . .?" "I've found the
Great Silence, and I've come to see that the noise
was inside!"[6]

Meditators on the Word of God have found the "Great Silence." It is the peaceful silence of entering boldly before the throne of God in the presence of our Great High Priest, Jesus. We wait silently. It is not a time of speaking, until God first speaks to us. We long to hear Him speak; the sound of His voice brings indescribable joy to our hearts.

Silence is important. We are so used to "getting up and going" that we feel guilty if we take time out to be silent. But silence is the key to hearing God speak. A heart wholly directed toward the Lord is a receptive heart. When God speaks, we are able to hear Him. Then God is able to share His heart for us and for the world, as we meditate on His Word.

Meditation is a time of solitude, resting in the healing presence of the Lord. It is a time of silence, maintaining an attitude of listening with a whole heart to all that God would like to say to us. This is the way the disciple begins each day in the Lord. The time does not have to be long. Many people with busy schedules can only spend fifteen or twenty minutes each day in meditation on the Word of God. But it will be a life-changing twenty minutes! Solitude and silence do not lead us away from the world; rather they lead us more deeply into the world. Sitting alone in the presence of God, listening in silence as He speaks to us through His word, transforms our lives by bringing us into knowledge of God and enabling us to receive His gift of compassion. Then we are free to minister to the world.

Invitation to the Banquet Table
Personal Meditation on Psalm 139

1. Review the four simple steps of meditation:
First, prepare your heart.
Second, listen to all God wants to say to you through the text.
Third, seek to meet God as He reveals Himself to you.
Fourth, respond to Him in prayer and obedience.

2. Read through the entire chapter of Psalm 139.
Open yourself to God and listen as you read.
Try to understand what the psalmist wants to express through this psalm.

3. Meditate on Psalm 139, **verse 3.**
You search out my path and my lying down
And are acquainted with all my ways.
Consider that the Lord knows you better than anyone else, even yourself.
He knows all your ways and wants to lead you in the paths of righteousness.
Listen to what the Lord wants to say to you personally!

4. Write down in your Meditation Journal what the Lord
says to you.
Or you may write out your prayer to Him.
Allow the Spirit to lead you as you listen to the Lord.

5. Take time now to *wait upon the Lord*.
Give Him your heart. Ask Him to reveal Himself to you.

5. Spend time in prayer.
Thank God for His word to you.
Commit yourself to obey Him.

Chapter Four

The Subject of Our Meditation

We have said that God is the subject of all our meditation. Our great desire as believers is to be so filled
with God in all His fullness of grace, love, holiness and
power that we are able to walk with Him in unbroken intimacy, keeping our eyes fixed on the One who is "always
before us."[1] "On the glorious splendor of Your majesty . . . I
will meditate," exclaims the psalmist. (Psalm 145:5)

God has provided various means to enable us to meditate on Him. All these means are precisely that: means, or
methods, to enable us to focus upon Him and to draw closer
into His presence and behold His radiance, becoming transformed by His loving gaze upon us. We should explore all
the ways God has revealed Himself: as Creator, in the world
of nature; as Lord of all time and history, in the events of
redemption and salvation; and above all through the written
Word, which is God's special revelation of Himself. And we
should expect to meet Him daily as we walk in communion
with Him.

Meditating On the Word of God

No method of meditation will draw us closer to God than the Word of God itself. Christian spirituality never goes beyond the Word of God. No higher state of meditation, or contemplation, exists which can take us to a more exalted level of spiritual maturity than the Word of God itself. Listen to the psalmist as he extols the Word of God:

> *My eyes are awake before the watches of the night, that I may meditate on your promise . . . . Even though princes sit plotting against me, your servant will meditate on your statutes. Your testimonies are my delight; they are my counselors . . . . Your statutes have been my songs in the house of my sojourning . . . . Oh how I love your law! It is my meditation all the day . . . . Your testimonies are my heritage forever, for they are the joy of my heart.[2]*

Daily meditation on the words of the Bible, the Word of God, will transform the faint-hearted Christian into a bold witness for God. Pausing before a single verse of Scripture, as we read or study, to prayerfully allow God to *meet* us in those few words, expecting Him to speak to us a word of grace that will equip us to minister to the weary ones who cross our paths each day — this is the meditation that changes lives and that eventually will change the world through our obedience.

Meditation on the Bible is powerful because the words of Scripture themselves lead us into the presence of Jesus Christ who is *the* Word of God. The first two stanzas of the hymn *Break Thou the Bread of Life*[3] reveal this truth clearly.

"Break Thou the bread of life, dear Lord, to me,
As Thou didst break the loaves beside the sea;
Beyond the sacred page I seek Thee, Lord.
My spirit longs for Thee, O living Word!

"Bless Thou the truth revealed this day to me,
As Thou didst bless the bread by Galilee.
Then shall all bondage cease, all fetters fall;
And *I shall find in Thee my all in all.*"

We seek Jesus! When we meditate on the Scriptures, the Spirit takes us beyond the printed page, into the presence of the Lord. And it is there that we find healing, release from bondages, and true satisfaction in Him.

Meditating On God Himself

Meditating on God Himself is very rewarding. The meditator would do well to study the nature and attributes of God, as well as the many aspects of His character. Many resources are available that will help the inquiring student know God more fully.[4] After understanding who God is—His eternal attributes and divine nature, His character—then we can join the psalmist in meditating upon God.

In his book *Knowing God,* Dr. J. I. Packer writes that in order to know God we must deal with three themes: First is the *Godhead* of God: the qualities that set God apart from humans, such as His self-existence, His infinity, His eternity, His unchangeableness. Second, we must understand His *powers:* His almightiness, His omniscience, and His omnipresence. Third, we must study His moral character or *perfections:* His holiness, His love and mercy, His faithfulness, His goodness, His patience, His justice.[5] Former generations considered these subjects to be so important that they included them in all basic training and discipleship. I remember having been required, as a teenager in Sunday School class, to memorize the Westminster Shorter Catechism. The fourth question is: "What is God?" And the answer is, "God is a Spirit, infinite, eternal, and unchangeable, in his being, wisdom, power, holiness, justice, goodness, and truth." Yet today most Christians are not aware of this way of talking about the nature and attributes of God. Some indeed will study and even meditate on the moral character of God, but few will attempt to understand the other aspects of the nature of God.

It was an especially tranquil, cool morning, and I was driving my Volkswagen Beetle on the small highway from Kona to Kealakakua on the Big Island of Hawaii. A refreshing morning rain shower had created a double rainbow in the sky and I was overwhelmed by the greatness and majesty of God. It was not the beauty of the heavens that captured my attention; rather it was the beauty of God Himself—the splendor of His majesty and the greatness of His being. As I pulled the car over to the side of the road, I became aware that I was in the presence of the all-knowing, all-powerful, ever-present God, Creator of all things. And I was welcomed into His presence! Such a small, sinful, seemingly insignificant creature, yet invited into His presence! Allowed to behold Him—the King of Glory, God of holiness and righteousness—because He extended His mercy and compassion to me as I turned my attention to Him and focused on His presence that morning!

Our God is approachable. Even a little child can enter into deep fellowship with God, and no repentant sinner is barred from communion with Him. One form of meditation is to take time to come apart from our daily affairs and focus on God Himself, just as the psalmist did: "My soul will be satisfied . . . and my mouth will praise you . . . when I remember you upon my bed, and meditate on you in the watches of the night; for you have been my help, and in the shadow of your wings I will sing for joy." (Psalm 63:5-7) Again the psalmist exclaims, "On the glorious splendor of your majesty . . . I will meditate." (Psalm 145:5)

A good way to meditate on God directly is to meditate on His nature and attributes or on His character. We can sit before the Lord or take a walk in His presence, and concentrate on His unchangeableness, His goodness, His love, His faithfulness, His justice, His holiness, or His omnipresence. This kind of meditation will be most effective if we do a parallel study of that aspect of God while meditating. Meditation and study go hand in hand. The more we spend time in diligent study about who God is, the deeper will be our meditation and the more intimate will be our fellowship with Him. And our meditation will increase our knowledge of God.

We may wish to study and meditate on God who is faithful. This is one way to do it: In our daily reading, each time we come across a verse of Scripture that speaks of God's faithfulness, we would write out that verse in our "Character of God Notebook."[6] We would continue to do this as we read through the Bible, for as long as we desire to meditate on the faithfulness of God. We should also make note of the evidences of God's faithfulness that we see in our daily lives, or in people we meet. After a few months, as we go back and meditate on each of those verses, or on those notes, we will discover that the God of faithfulness is revealing Himself to us in new and intimate ways. Our renewed trust in His faithfulness will cause our faith to increase, and we will find that we ourselves are becoming more faithful in our Christian walk.

Meditating On the Works of Salvation

Meditation on the works of salvation will bring great comfort and security to the believer. Although we may *understand* how God has "created a people with whom He can dwell," through the Cross and Resurrection of His Son, nevertheless we begin to *experience* the richness and depths of our salvation only as we meditate on those works. "One generation shall commend your works to another, and shall declare your mighty acts. On . . . your wondrous works I will meditate," sings the psalmist. "All your works shall give thanks to you, O Lord, and all your saints shall bless you . . . and will make known to the children of man your mighty deeds, and the glorious splendor of your kingdom!"[7]

What are the "works of salvation?" The wondrous work of God in Christ when He reconciled the world unto Himself through the Cross, the shedding of the blood of the sinless Christ for sinners' welfare, the tomb left empty by the Spirit's raising Jesus from the dead, the descent of the Spirit at Pentecost to empower Christ's Church for life and ministry.

Every disciple of Jesus Christ should consistently meditate on the cross, on the blood that He shed for the redemption of mankind, and on His resurrection. The angels and all celestial beings in heaven continually praise the Lamb who was slain before the foundation of the world, and their songs of praise are focused mainly on the blood of the Lamb. It is their meditation as they proclaim His works.[8] How fitting, then, for God's people on earth to focus our minds on the finished work of God in Christ on the cross of Calvary.

We can meditate also on the works that *preceded* the saving act of God on the Cross: God's deliverance of His people from bondage and the miraculous rescue at the Red Sea and supernatural feeding in the wilderness; the reconstituting of God's people after seventy years of exile; the sending of John the Baptist to herald the Messiah's coming; the divine intervention of God in history in the form of a helpless baby.

Meditating on God's works of salvation *after* the Cross and Resurrection will also provide rich materials for meditation. We can meditate on the powerful community of the Spirit in the Book of Acts, or on God's interruption of Saul's self-satisfying life of religiosity and His transforming him into the most powerful witness for Christ the world has ever known. How rich would be our meditation on the lives of the saints recorded in the eleventh chapter of Hebrews! And nothing could surpass time spent in focusing all our attention, both mind and heart, on the Final Coming of our Lord Jesus Christ!

Remember as you meditate, that God wants to meet you and speak to you personally. Take time to kneel before the cross in a beautiful chapel, or visualize in your mind the blood of Jesus, which contains His life. Contemplate His deliverance of His people at the Exodus, or His deliverance of you from a life of sin and shame, or from a tragedy that would have ended your life. Meditate on His miraculous provision for you when you had no way to provide for your family or for your necessary expenses. Consider and ponder deeply God's divine guidance for you, which has brought you to your present commitment. Meditate on God's works by which He reveals His righteousness, His kindness and goodness. Remember what He has done for you. Expect Him to continue to be faithful to His character, and to fulfill all His promises.

We see God's works of righteousness and goodness not only through the words of Scripture, but also at times through His people who serve Him, often without the praise of others. We find such people among the unsung saints who minister to the dying in AIDS hospices, or among those brave believers who boldly go to war-torn countries as advocates for peace and reconciliation, or in the considerate widow who cares for her mentally unstable neighbor and treats her with dignity.

Meditating On God's Creation

One of the most pleasurable and life-changing methods of meditating on God is to meditate on His creation, His handiworks of nature. A mark of the Psalms is the awe and wonder of the psalmist as he beholds God's creation, such as David when he said, "When I look at your heavens, the work of your fingers, the moon and the stars, which you have set in place, what is man that you are mindful of him?" (Psalm 8:3-4a) Even now I can recall my junior high school days, lying flat on my back on an old pier at our church's campground during a summer retreat. The pier extended no more than fifty feet onto the lake, but we managed to fit our entire junior high church group into that small area. Even the pastor[9] found a place to lie there with us for what seemed to be hours, as we remained speechless (no small feat for a rowdy bunch!), gazing into the starry heavens and meditating on the Lord who calls every star by name. We later would share our sense of awe and wonder, or anything else we thought about or felt, as we warmed ourselves by the campfire drinking hot chocolate.

The psalmist tells us that the heavens themselves are God's great missionaries, that their "speechless speech" and "wordless voices" go throughout the earth, day and night, proclaiming who God is. (Psalm 19:1-6) Paul the Apostle later told the Christians of Rome that everyone, even pagans, are accountable to God. "For his invisible attributes, namely, his eternal power and divine nature, have been clearly perceived, ever since the creation of the world, *in the things that have been made. So they are without excuse.*" (Romans 1:20) If God reveals Himself through nature even to non-believers, would it not follow that meditation on nature would be a powerful way to experience God and hear Him as He speaks to us?

George MacDonald described how God's Spirit moves in the hearts of non-believers to cause them to draw near to God through the beauties of nature. Speaking of a young man who had not yet found God, he wrote:

> *He began to feel his heart drawn at times, in some strange, tender fashion previously unknown to him, to the blue of the sky, especially in the first sweetness of a summer morning. His soul would now and then seem to go out of him, in a passion of embrace, to the simplest flower. He would spread out his arms to the wind, now when it met him in its strength, now when it kissed his face. He never admitted to himself that it was **one force in all the forms** that drew him—that perhaps it was the very God, the All in all about him... All the time a divine power of truth and beauty had laid hold upon him, and was working in him as only the powers of God can work in a man.*[10]

"One force in all the forms" describes well what God intends to happen in meditation. God reveals Himself through many forms, even in nature itself. We meditate on God through the forms of nature, or through the method of sitting before His Word and listening to Him, or by using other methods. But it is *one force*—the force of God's Spirit—that draws our souls into the presence of God, who alone is the subject of all Christian meditation.

A young man in Japan had an experience similar to the fictional young man in George MacDonald's novel. He was very much troubled in his spirit and tended to avoid people as much as possible, so he had few meaningful personal relationships. His deeply wounded spirit made him unapproachable to most people. But he attended a meditation seminar in which the participants were each given a beautiful red rose on which to meditate. As he picked up his rose his eyes went immediately to the thorns, for that was how he saw himself—full of thorns, wounds, unresolved conflicts. He held the rose loosely, his hands wrapped around the thorns, and that seemed to be the essence of his meditation on the rose. Later, however, during a time of sharing, he said that although at first he could not take his eyes off the thorns he gradually began to gaze upon the exquisite beauty of the crimson red rose. It was at that point that Jesus revealed himself to this young man. He confessed that he felt as though he were looking directly at the shed blood of Jesus, the blood that covered all his sins and removed all his thorns. He had an experience with Jesus that transformed his life simply by meditating on a rose for thirty minutes! This meditation, together with the loving care he received from others in the community that sponsored the seminar, led to his full recovery from his wounded spirit. Today he is a pastor of a church in Japan, who loves his people and is easily approached even by small children. His meditation on God is the key to his fruitful life.

Multitudes of people around the world have similar stories of how God has touched them, or revealed Himself to them, as they walked along a beach at sunset and fixed their eyes upon the radiant colors of the setting sun, or as they stood watching the gentle waves beat steadily against the rocks, each wave a sign of God's abundant grace and love. Who could stand at the top of a majestic mountain peak overlooking valleys and rivers, all signs of God's creation, and not want to sing out at the top of his voice, "Then sings my soul, my Savior, God, to Thee, how great Thou art! How great Thou art!"?

But Thomas Merton said it best, when he described his experiences at sunrise.

Sunrise! It is an event that calls forth solemn music in the very depths of man's nature, as if one's whole being had to attune itself to the cosmos and praise God for the new day, praise him in the name of all the creatures that ever were or will ever be. I look at the rising sun and feel that now upon me falls the responsibility of seeing what all my ancestors have seen . . . praising God before me. Whether or not they praised him then, for themselves, they must praise him now in me. When the sun rises each one of us is summoned by the living and the dead to praise God.[11]

Even secular studies have indicated that meditation on nature contributes to relief from stress in modern society. Stephen Kaplan, a professor of psychology at the University of Michigan, was part of a group that did research on mental fatigue. He spoke of the group's research findings, saying, "The essential factor [in mental health] is the capacity to focus one's attention, and when that starts to deteriorate there are a whole series of difficulties that arise. It's difficult to listen to somebody else, to make effective decisions; there's a tendency to be impatient and impulsive, to get on with it, rather than consider alternatives. There's a tendency that goes against being reflective or being thoughtful."

The single most powerful antidote to mental fatigue, he says, is to focus on the *natural environment*, "even looking out the window into the natural environment." Studies have shown that cancer patients recover faster, prison inmates stay healthier, and people experience less work pressure when they have a window view of nature. "*For reasons no one quite understands* [italics mine], a view of trees is an extremely powerful factor," he concludes.[12]

This is exactly what meditation does. As we meditate we focus our attention on God, as He reveals Himself through the beauty of His creation, and through His Word. As we learn to focus more fully on God, we become whole, we become healed. We begin to walk in the footsteps of the great meditator Enoch, who "walked with God," continually consumed by His presence, becoming more like Him each step of the way.

A Lesson from Meditation On Nature

A few years ago, Ellen and I had the privilege of visiting missionaries in Tanzania. Besides participating in ministry and enjoying fellowship with all the missionaries there, Jaeson Choi, one of the long-term missionaries, took us on a safari. This is how Ellen described the trip.

> *The vast crater is home to various species of wild life. Water buffaloes, wildebeests, lions, hyenas, zebras and flamingo were among the ones we saw that unforgettable day. As we drove we noticed other vehicles stopped, watching a pair of lionesses stalking a lone zebra. The animals were oblivious to those of us watching just a stone's throw away. We watched and waited quietly for an hour or so while the zebra grazed and the lionesses, hidden by the tall grass, very slowly approached their prey. Some distance away the herd of zebras were grazing, evidently unaware of the lone zebra's plight.*
> *Suddenly one of the lionesses pounced, startling but missing the zebra who then quickly ran to join the herd. Immediately three larger, stately zebras took the lone zebra's place,*

standing together shoulder to shoulder less than twenty feet away from the lionesses. They stared at the two lionesses, who meekly retreated.

It was quite an impressive sight. Such a drama surely would have meaning for us, so as I meditated on this wondrous event of nature I asked the Lord for insight.

I believe the herd was like a body of believers, often oblivious to the vulnerability of its members. The lone zebra reminded me of a Christian who drifts away, neglecting the fellowship and nurture of the community.

The three stallion zebras who came out to stand against the attackers made me think of our responsibility as intercessors to "stand in the gap," by praying for and helping brothers and sisters who are in crisis.

God made my meditation very practical to me, because at the time our family had been praying for one of our members who was going through a crisis. I was comforted, knowing God was in control and would receive glory as we came through that difficult time more strengthened and full of hope than we could have imagined. How faithful is our God!

Guidelines for Meditation

All these various forms of meditation will bring the believer into a deeper knowledge of God and more intimate fellowship with Him. God reveals Himself in many ways, and He desires us to see Him and meet Him in all areas of our lives.

The Apostle Paul gives clear guidelines for the meditating Christian in his letter to the Philippian Christians. After exhorting them to seek the peace of God by rejoicing in the Lord, by praying instead of worrying, and by being thankful, he then gives them guidelines for maintaining that peace. These are in fact guidelines for meditation.

"Finally, brothers, whatever is true, whatever is honorable, whatever is just, whatever is pure, whatever is lovely, whatever is commendable, if there is any excellence, if there is anything worthy of praise, think about these things." (Philippians 4:8) The New Jerusalem Bible says, "Let your minds *be filled*" with these things. J.B. Phillips, in his paraphrase of the New Testament, says, "*Fix your mind*" on such things. Clearly, Paul is telling us to meditate on things we see, on the beauty we see in people around us, or on events that happen in our lives that reveal the purity, the loveliness, the justice, and the excellence of God.

The meditator expects to meet God each day, to behold His wonders and beauty and to walk in ever deepening communion with Him. God has provided the means of grace for us to behold Him and to be transformed by Him. May His Spirit grant us increasing sensitivity that we may see Him when He comes to us.

Invitation to the Banquet Table
Personal Meditation on Psalm 139

1. Review the four simple steps of meditation:
First, prepare your heart.
Second, listen to all God wants to say to you through the
text.
Third, seek to meet God as He reveals Himself to you.
Fourth, respond to Him in prayer and obedience.

2. Read through the entire chapter of Psalm 139.
Open yourself to God and listen as you read.
Try to understand what the psalmist wants to express
through this psalm.

3. Meditate on Psalm 139, **verse 4.**
*Even before a word is on my tongue, behold, O Lord, you
know it altogether.*
God knows your innermost thoughts.
He knows the words you will speak.
Ask Him to speak to you about the way you speak to
others.
Listen to what the Lord wants to say to you personally!

4. Write down in your Meditation Journal what the Lord
says to you.
Or you may write out your prayer to Him.
Allow the Spirit to lead you as you listen to the Lord.

5. Take time now to *wait upon the Lord*.
Give Him your heart. Ask Him to reveal Himself to you.

6. Spend time in prayer.
Thank God for His word to you.
Commit yourself to obey Him.

Part Two

The Transforming Word

God's Word always transforms the hearer.
His Spirit plants God's Word
in my inner being as I meditate
and listen to Him,
just as a farmer plants seeds
for his harvest.

As I respond to the Lord,
who awakens my ear each morning
to listen as a disciple,
God, through His Word,
awakens faith
deep within my soul.
Then God begins
to use me as a nation changer.

Chapter Five

The Seed Is the Word

"The Seed is the word of God."
Luke 8:11

The decisive question for the student of the Bible is: How does the Word of God come into the believer's life? The Scriptures tell us that we should "abide" in the Word, that the Word of God desires to take up residence in the life of the Christian. Jesus Himself promises us that "if you abide in Me, and My words abide in you, ask whatever you wish, and it will be done for you." (John 15:7) The meditator must ask the question: How is it possible for the words of Christ to make their home in us?

God's Word Is a Seed.

Jesus told a parable about a farmer who went out to sow seed. As he sowed, some seed fell along the path and was trampled and immediately destroyed. Some fell on rocks and withered for lack of moisture. Other seed fell among thorns and weeds and was choked, producing no fruit. But some seed fell on good ground and produced abundant fruit.

Jesus' disciples could not understand the parable, so He explained it to them. In doing so, Jesus revealed perhaps the greatest truth a meditator needs to know: "The seed is the word of God!" (Luke 8:11) Here is the answer to our question, as well as the secret of meditation! Indeed this is a key reason Christians throughout twenty centuries of Church history have found meditation on the Bible to be one of the most dynamic resources for spiritual transformation and growth. The secret is this: the words of Scripture are in fact *seeds*, which the Holy Spirit plants in the hearts of listening Christians!

As the Spirit of God plants the seeds of the Word in our lives, that word of course enters my head through my intellectual faculties. But it does not stop there! It goes beyond my head—beyond simple human understanding and intellectual knowledge—and is planted in my heart. From my head into my heart! We do not lose the knowledge we have of God, which we have acquired through our human reason and which itself is a gift from God. Instead, the Word of God enters my inner being and takes up residence there. And my knowledge *about* God becomes knowledge *of* God. Meditation is the bridge that takes us from mere intellectual *knowledge about God* to intimate *knowledge of Him*.

It is said that the farthest distance in the world is the distance between the head and the heart. Some Christians never complete the journey. May you, dear reader, come to know Jesus Christ not only with your mind but also with your heart, as you begin the journey of meditating on His Word. May you be like those of whom Christ Himself said, " . . . who, hearing the word, *hold it fast in an honest and good heart,* and bear fruit with patience." (Luke 8:15) But to bear fruit as Christ said, we must examine more closely the concept of the Word of God as a seed!

The DNA of a Seed

Walking through the giant redwood forests of northern California, one is overwhelmed at the majesty of those centuries-old trees. But more remarkable indeed is the fact that each gigantic tree comes from a single seed. Nearly negligible when placed beside the tree, the seed nevertheless contains the DNA of the entire tree. All that the tree eventually will become already exists within that one tiny seed.

The year 2002 was the 50th anniversary of the discovery of DNA—deoxyribonucleic acid. This was an astounding discovery that helped begin the new science of biotechnology, provided the foundation for understanding the diversity of life on earth, opened the door to gene therapy, shed light on diseases such as cancer, and made possible forensic evidence for the solving of crimes. How ironic, though, that the two scientists who made this discovery, James Watson and Francis Crick, both used that anniversary to launch an attack on religion, even suggesting that their discovery has made God "unnecessary." In particular, they attacked the idea that "truth comes from divine revelation."

But the Telegraph of London, which publicized the anniversary of this discovery, actually refuted the two renown scientists and advised its readers not to be "taken in by their irreligious hubris." The newspaper then gave extensive coverage of the work of the scientist who succeeded James Watson in 1993, Francis Collins. Dr. Collins, a devout Christian, complained that God received a "cold reception" during the 50th anniversary celebrations. He told the Telegraph he was concerned that the anti-religious views of these "very distinguished figures" will increase public antipathy to genetics, and hastened to add that Watson and Crick do not represent all scientists.

On the contrary, he said, religion and science complement and mutually support one another. His own research to discover the faulty gene responsible for cystic fibrosis "provided scientific exhilaration," he said, "and a sense of awe at uncovering something that God knew before that we humans didn't."[1]

Perhaps more remarkable is the fact that the Telegraph of London went on to point out that the great significance of the discovery of DNA was that the very core of life is information, and "all that information could not have come about by chance in a random universe." Rather, to use the Telegraph's own words, it "can only be the work of a Designer!"

The Designer of Our Lives

God, the "Great Designer" of the universe and all its inhabitants, is the one who allowed the discovery of DNA. He delights in revealing the intricacies of His plans and designs to the earnest seeker, even to a non-Christian, because all truth is His. Rather than "making God unnecessary," these discoveries cause us to stand in greater awe and wonder at God's mysteries. They create within us the desire to worship Him.

Careful research enabled scientists to discover the DNA of the human body. But what about the soul, the spirit of man, that which makes us really human? How do we know what we are made of, what is each individual's unique identity and formation? Where can we find out about our past, and about our future?

The answer is, only in the Word of God. God's written Word, the Bible, contains the believer's "spiritual DNA!" God's Spirit plants the seed of the Word in my inner being as I meditate. Just as the tiny seed of a majestic redwood tree contains the DNA of that tree, so the seed of God's Word will reveal to me all that I am as a spiritual being. The Word reveals the source of my life. God Himself formed my inward parts; He knitted me together in my mother's womb.

The Word further reveals my uniqueness. I am "fearfully and wonderfully made!" (Psalm 139:14) Scripture also tells us that we are "born again, not of perishable seed but of imperishable, through the living and abiding word of God." (1 Peter 1:23) The Word of God contains the truth about the source of my life, about my identity and about my destiny.

The Holy Spirit Plants Jesus, the Word.

The Apostle John tells us that Jesus Himself is *the* Word of God. He begins his Gospel by stating, "In the beginning was the Word." The Holy Spirit "planted" the seed, Jesus, the Word, in Mary. And He also plants Jesus, the Word, in us. We live our lives by abiding in Him. "Whoever abides in me and I in him," says Jesus, "he it is that bears much fruit, for apart from Me you can do nothing." (John 15:5)

The Holy Spirit Plants the Words of Jesus.

One secret of abiding is that the Spirit who "plants" Jesus, the Word, in us also plants the *words* of Jesus in us. And it is in these words that we discover our "spiritual DNA!" Here indeed is the basic reason that our meditation must be on the Word of God itself, and not on devotional books that explain or comment on that Word. The Word of God planted within us by the Spirit of God contains our eternal origins and our eternal destiny.

We must always remember that meditation is not just mentally appropriating the ideas of a text, or the meaning of that text, into our lives. Meditation is not just understanding, not just reading, not even "spiritual reading." No, meditation is *allowing the Holy Spirit to plant the seed of the Word in me!*

Meditating on the Word of God goes beyond merely reading, studying or memorizing the Bible. We know that reading God's Word provides the solid foundation for the Christian's life, which enables him to hear God's truth and understand His message of salvation. The true believer constantly desires to read the Scriptures in order to be immersed in God's truth. And of course true discipleship demands a thorough study of God's Word, so that the believer can understand and apply that Word to his life and teach others. Moreover those who live the victorious life in Christ realize the great importance of memorizing key passages of the Bible. "Do your best to present yourself to God as one approved," Paul exhorted Timothy, "a worker who has no need to be ashamed, rightly handling the word of truth." (2 Timothy 2:15)

But God has provided a special feast for those Christians who read, study and memorize God's Word, and who seek to go deeper into His presence and be renewed by His Word. That is the feast of meditation. Jesus would say to the seeking Christian, "Come, feast with Me! My banquet table is prepared for you!"

We are transformed as we sit each morning with Jesus before the feast of His Word. Not instantaneously, but gradually, piecemeal, but without question transformed. The Holy Spirit enables the meditator, "with unveiled face . . . to behold the glory of the Lord," and to enter into the presence of the Lord to be "transformed into the same image from one degree of glory to another." (2 Corinthians 3:18) Our minds are renewed, our emotions healed, our wills redirected, our hungry hearts nourished. And the great tool that the Spirit uses to do this is meditation on the Word of God!

Each time I meditate on a verse of scripture, the Holy Spirit *plants the seed of that word in my heart!* The word of God then *resides* inside me and becomes active to produce in me God's total salvation for my spirit, emotions, mind, will and body.

Receiving the Word

"Therefore put away all filthiness and rampant wicked-ness and receive with meekness the implanted word, which is able to save your souls." (James 1:21) Thus spoke the Apostle James, as he instructed his readers to practice true faith by turning away from anger, and instead receiving and acting upon the Word of God. James then promised that the one who "looks into the perfect law of liberty," that is, the whole Word of God, will be blessed and become a truly godly, or spiritual, person. (James 1:22-27)

How simple yet revolutionary is this truth. The seed is the Word! Each time we open our hearts to God's Word, the Spirit of God plants it deeply into our inner beings, word-by-word, line-by-line. Just as a good farmer tills the soil in the springtime and then plants the seed for the late summer harvest, so the Spirit plants the seed of the Word into our hearts, that we may bear fruit in due season.

A heart patient may have a heart transplant. A person suffering from kidney disorder may require a kidney trans-plant. Such miracles of modern medicine have saved the lives of many people and enabled them to live productive lives.

But God desires all Christians to have a *Word implant!* He wants His Word to dwell richly within us, filling us with all the fullness of God Himself. This is the only way we can live fruitful, productive lives. But how can this happen? The Great Physician Himself will insert the implant!

How to Receive the Implanted Word

How can we "receive the implanted word?" Dietrich Bonhoeffer, who uniquely embraced both a deep spirituality and a strong biblical sense of social justice, gives us this clue: "If the Word is to be implanted in us and if the purpose of this implanting is to save our souls, we are talking about a subjective experience of the Word and not mere critical knowledge."[2]

Bonhoeffer points out that many Bible scholars, as well as seminarians, attempt to make the Bible into a mere *historical* document which they then approach with a scholarly detachment, and in so doing actually prevent the Scriptures from being God's living Word to themselves and to their people.

Although the Bible is the objective Word of God, nevertheless the Christian can never approach the Bible from a purely objective viewpoint. Who can be objective before the God who loves us passionately and sacrificially and who demands our total allegiance? Who can distance himself to look only "critically" at the God who asks simply, "Do you love Me?" Of course the Bible is God's objective truth. But when that Word enters us, we must subjectively experience the *implanted Word* that the Spirit places inside us.

James tells us that we must become "doers of the Word;" we must allow the Word of God to re-shape us, becoming men and women of God who are "formed by the Word" in order to bring His life to our generation. He points the way: turn away from sin and evil; redirect your life to God; live a lifestyle that is going in God's direction rather than in the direction of sin. The text further points to the way in which one should receive it. "Receive with meekness (or humility) the implanted word." (James 1:21) The Greek word in this text has been translated either as "humility" or as "meekness." We must examine both words.

Receiving the Implanted Word With Humility

Humility is without exception the key Christian virtue. It was the mark of Jesus Christ, who humbled Himself, leaving the glories of heaven to partake of a human body and take the sins of the whole world upon Himself. Yet humility is perhaps the most misunderstood of all the Christian virtues. Even Christians have understood it to be anything from shyness or awkwardness to self-mutilation of the body. What, then, is true Christian humility?

"Apart from God, I am nothing and can do nothing," is where we begin. Humility is to come to the Lord "poor in spirit," which actually means that I am spiritually bankrupt as I stand before God; I have nothing to offer Him. Yet the beautiful paradox of humility is that when I come to God in this way, I become a vessel able to contain the Spirit of God Himself! I become nothing so that God can become everything in me. The Triune God—Father, Son and Holy Spirit— uses me as His channel through which He can allow all His blessings and gifts to flow to the world. So I confess with the Apostle Paul that, even though I am nothing in myself, nevertheless I am *"God's work of art;"* (Ephesians 2:10a New Jerusalem Bible), and "I can do all things through Him who strengthens me!" (Philippians 4:13)

When we come to the Lord in humility we come in total availability to Him to be used as He desires. This makes it possible for God's Spirit to perform His *unlimited ministry* through us, because it is Christ Himself in us who is doing His ministry through us by the power of His Holy Spirit. Then we give God all the glory.

Is this not a powerful way to ask the Spirit to plant the Word of God in our inner person as we meditate? We come before the Word humbly, confessing that we can do nothing unless He works in us and that we have nothing to say unless He first speaks to us. So we listen to God as He speaks to us through the Word. He speaks. We listen and obey. We say to God that we are totally available to Him to use us as He desires, anywhere, at any time and in any place. As we listen, God's Spirit implants His Word deeply into our souls. We are ready to be used by Him and to give Him all the glory.

This is the humility of which God spoke through the prophet Isaiah: "But this is the one to whom I will look: he who is humble and contrite in spirit and trembles at My word!" (Isaiah 66:2b) This describes the basic character trait of the meditator: approaching the Word of God in deep humility.

Receiving the Implanted Word With Meekness

The same word that is often translated as *humility* in James 1:21 has been rendered in the Korean Bible as *gentleness,* or *meekness.* The meditator must approach the Word in a spirit of meekness, or gentleness.

We must approach the Word of God in the two attitudes that Jesus Himself said were His own two chief character traits: humility and meekness (gentleness). In that greatest of all Scriptural invitations, Jesus cries out to the spiritually and physically oppressed crowds, "Come to Me, all who labor and are heavy laden, and I will give you rest!" (Matthew 11:28-30) He then continues, "Take my yoke upon you, and learn from Me, for I am meek and lowly (or humble) in heart." Humility and meekness, two character traits of Jesus Himself, are the essential character traits of those who meditate on His Word!

Kim Ki-Chang, known also by his pen name, Oonbo, was a famous painter whom I admired greatly in Korea. His greatest appeal was the masterful way in which he could paint large wall-sized paintings of wild horses, leaping and jumping on the canvas with unrestrained power and might. My Korean language teacher, Mrs. Hedi Hahm, introduced me to this wonderful painter, as well as to many other important areas of Korea's culture, and I recall sitting before his paintings for hours, in awe at the brilliance with which he captured the raw power and exhilarating strength of those massive untamed beasts.

As I learned to appreciate his paintings, I discovered that in classical Greek the word for "meek," or "gentle," carries the meaning of a wild horse that has been tamed to obey even the gentlest command of its owner. Power is not taken away from the horse; it is merely redirected to its owner's wishes. The meek Christian is one whose will is redirected towards God; one who "prefers God's will" above his own. To receive the Word implanted with *meekness* means to *submit* one's self without reservation to God who speaks to us through His Word, to completely yield ourselves to Him and allow Him to reshape us according to that word which will remold our thought patterns, our emotions, our will.

When we give ourselves in submission to God in His Word, He then gives us the power to love Him to the point of joyfully sacrificing ourselves for those people He brings into our lives for us to serve. When we begin to meditate on the Word with a heart of submission we will find that meditation, far from removing us from the world, will drive us deeper into the world with a sacrificial spirit to minister to the lonely, the outcast and lost.

Moses was such a man. "The meekest man who ever lived," is how the Old Testament describes him. Moses gave up his rights to all the treasures of Egypt, which would have been available to him if he had so desired. He chose rather to submit himself to God without reservation and by so doing received grace from God to sacrifice himself for his people. As meditators today we are surrounded by Moses and all that other great cloud of witnesses who cheer us on as we run the race that is set before us.

Four Things I Must Do

The person who decides to plant seeds in order to enjoy a good harvest must consider many things. The soil must be the right kind of soil, and it must be prepared. The timing of planting is important, and care for the young seedling as it grows is crucial to producing the desired result. So it is with the seed that is planted in our hearts! Andrew Murray suggests that there are four things one must do if he desires the Holy Spirit to plant the seed of God's Word in him: First, he must receive the Word by faith. Second, he must work to prepare for the seed. Third, he must be patient and allow the Word to abide in him. Fourth, he must believe that the Word in him will bear fruit.[3] Let us consider the implications of these four steps.

First, I must receive the Word by faith. Paul thanked the believers of Thessalonica for accepting the word that he proclaimed to them "not as the word of men but *as what it really is, the word of God."* (1 Thessalonians 2:13) Later, when he gave his farewell discourse to the elders of the Ephesian Church, Paul did not commend the Word of God to the believers, but rather the believers to the Word of God! He did this because he knew that God's Word is more powerful than human strength. That Word is "able to build you up and to give you the inheritance among all those who are sancti-fied." (Acts 20:32)

I must receive the Word upon which I meditate each morning as God's Word to me, not as my own thought or as a human idea. I must trust that this Word contains God's purpose for me, for this day; that this Word will cleanse me, remold me, empower me, comfort me, equip me, feed me, to be God's "letter to the world."

Just as when one plants a tomato seed in the ground he expects it to produce good fruit to satisfy the taste, so as I receive the implanted Word that the Spirit gives to me each morning I must believe that this Word will work in me today all that God has planned for it to do. Then I must be ready to obey that Word.

Second, I must work to allow the Spirit to plant God's seed in me. Just as a farmer must work hard to cultivate the soil and make it ready for the seed, so I must cultivate my mind and heart to receive God's Word. I must desire it as a treasure more precious and valuable than anything I possess. I must welcome the Word with my whole heart. Meditation is actually receiving the Word of God with my whole heart—mind, will and emotions. I must listen actively and wholeheartedly. I must love that Word, desire it, embrace it, surrender my will to it, and yield my entire life to that Word with readiness to obey. This is the work I must do to receive God's Word. Meditation is *receiving the Word of God with my heart, in wholehearted submission, so I can live it out in my life.*

Receiving God's Word indeed is hard work. Yet as we prepare our hearts to receive that Word, God Himself promises us that this Word will bring transformation to our lives and equip us to serve Him in the world.

Third, I must be patient and allow the seed of God's Word to abide in me. The seed must remain in the ground if it is to produce fruit. Is it not reasonable then that the Word must remain in me, if God is to produce His fruit in my life? Indeed, God's great desire for Christians is that the Word of Christ dwell in us richly, so that we can live with one another in harmony and mutual encouragement, always thankful to God, never ceasing to praise Him. (Colossians 3:16)

I must allow the Holy Spirit to *hide* me in the Word. The prophet Isaiah wrote concerning the Suffering Servant, that God "made my mouth like a sharp sword; *in the shadow of His hand He hid me.* He made me a polished arrow; *in His quiver He hid me away."* (Isaiah 49:2) As believers we must take time to live in the Word. Rather than simply using it as a tool to do our own ministry, we must allow God's Word to rest in us until it does its work. God desires at times to *hide* us in His Word so that the Word can take root deep in our inner beings. Dear reader, can you see the uniqueness of meditation as a gift God wants to give you to equip you to be His servant in the world? There are times when God must even take us into the "desert," in order to give time for His Word to work within us. Do not despise these desert experiences, these times of loneliness and imagined distance from the Lord. It is simply the Lord hiding you in His Word, to perfect and equip you.

Fourth, I must believe that the Word implanted in me will bear fruit. God has promised: I will become a fruit-bearing Christian if I meditate. The meditator is like a "tree planted by streams of water that yields its fruit in its season." (Psalm 1:3)

The Word in me may be hidden so deeply by the Spirit that I even forget that it is there, inside me. But I must remember that, even though it may be slow to surface, it will indeed bear fruit in my life. But I must *depend upon that Word, trust it and commit my life to it!* God's Word will never fail me nor leave me desolate. I must remember God's promises: "It is *God* who works in you, both to will and to work for His good pleasure." (Philippians 2:13) Our fruit comes from Him alone. (Hosea 14:8) And our fruit will remain.

Knowing then that God plants His Word in us through His Holy Spirit, we now must examine more specifically the way in which He does it.

Invitation to the Banquet Table
Personal Meditation on Psalm 139

1. Review the four simple steps of meditation:
First, prepare your heart.
Second, listen to all God wants to say to you through the text.
Third, seek to meet God as He reveals Himself to you.
Fourth, respond to Him in prayer and obedience.

2. Read through the entire chapter of Psalm 139.
Open yourself to God and listen as you read.
Try to understand what the psalmist wants to express through this psalm.

3. Meditate on Psalm 139, **verse 5.**
You hem me in, behind and before, and lay your hand upon me.
God does not "hem you in" in order to limit you.
He "hems you in" to enable you to live within His boundaries of love.
He lays His hand upon you to bless and anoint you.
Listen to what the Lord wants to say to you personally!

4. Write down in your Meditation Journal what the Lord
says to you.
Or you may write out your prayer to Him.
Allow the Spirit to lead you as you listen to the Lord.

5. Take time now to *wait upon the Lord.*
Give Him your heart. Ask Him to reveal Himself to you.

6. Spend time in prayer.
Thank God for His word to you.
Commit yourself to obey Him.

Chapter Six

Planting the Seed Through Daily Meditation

"He awakens my ear . . . "
Isaiah 50:4

I saiah the prophet tells us that the people of Israel had lost all hope during their long years of Babylonian captivity. In their misery they thought that God had completely forsaken and deserted them, that He had "divorced their mother" and "sold them to creditors." (Isaiah 50:1-3) Having lost their nationhood and their freedom to worship in ways that had been familiar to them, they concluded that they were forgotten by God and totally helpless in their imprisonment.

But Isaiah reminded them that what was most important was how they saw and understood their captivity. His words still ring true for those of us who suffer today. Whether our imprisonment is due to persecution, sickness or loneliness, his words bring strong encouragement: "Awake, awake, put on your strength, O Zion . . . shake yourself from the dust and arise . . . loose the bonds from your neck, O captive daughter of Zion!" (Isaiah 52:1-2) Even in the midst of our captivity and suffering, we must never lose hope. We must trust God even during the "dark night of the soul," even when we cannot meet Him or hear Him speak.

Nevertheless God's people of Israel could not hear his words. Perhaps they *would* not hear the prophet's words. They saw themselves as victims. And their "victim mentality" caused them to angrily accuse God of deserting them. Surely we understand well Israel's plight. How many times have we cried out in our pain and anguish, "Where was God when I suffered so greatly? Why did He not come to me when I cried out night and day?"

God's reply must have been perplexing to Israel, as it may be to some today. He asked them, "Where is your mother's certificate of divorce to prove I sent her away?" Of course there was no certificate of divorce. He continued, "Indeed I did separate myself from you for a season because of your sin, but I never completely severed my relationship with you. I never left you, I was continually coming to you, calling out to you." Israel asked the question that many of us continue to ask: "Where were you, God, when I was suffering so greatly?" God's reply was: "Where were *you* when I came to you? Why, when I came, was there no man? Why, when I called, was there no one to answer?" (Isaiah 50:2) God was asking why there was no one at home when He came to visit!

The Christian's Home

Where, after all, is the Christian's home? Where was Israel's true home? No place other than the heart of God! God's heart is my home! Suffering in the world is temporary, for a season; God's love is permanent, without beginning or end. Jesus himself told his disciples that He would not leave them as orphans, never desert or forsake them. "Abide in Me, and I in you," said Jesus. (John 15:4) Our home is in the

Lord, and Satan himself can never remove us from God's strong love.

Abiding in the Lord is not a vague spiritual experience. Here lies one of the most important spiritual truths we must learn as Christians. *Spirituality never goes beyond hearing and obeying the Word of God.* Even in our deepest distress or times of sorrow, we still must keep ourselves in the presence of God by *listening to God in His Word!* "If you abide in Me, and My words abide in you, ask whatever you wish, and it will be done for you," said Jesus. (John 15:7) Yes, the Christian's home is the heart of God, and we abide in God by abiding in His Word! The Bible gives no instructions or guidelines for those who wish to abide in the presence of the Lord in a vague manner. The only way is to go daily into the "council of the Lord" and tune our ears to listen to Him as faithful disciples.

The Song of the Suffering Servant

The Book of Isaiah contains four "Suffering Servant Songs" which prophesy about the life of the coming Messiah, Jesus Christ.[1] These songs provide the Church with a clear understanding of the lifestyle and ministry of Jesus, the Suffering Servant, and also of the lifestyle and ministry of all those Jesus calls to be His servants. The third song, in Isaiah 50:4-9, which we will now examine, speaks of the Servant who listens to and obeys God completely, in stark contrast to the masses of people who cannot see beyond their own dilemma and who consequently cannot accept their own freedom in God.

God Awakens Me Each Morning.

The servant's life begins anew each morning, as God awakens him to a new day. Our life as servants of God is completely dependent on God who gives us breath. Were God not to awaken us in the morning, no other power in the universe could awaken us. Each day, then, as we are awakened, we respond to God in deep gratitude for His choice to give us life one more day; indeed we rejoice and celebrate this day: "This is the day the Lord has made; let us rejoice and be glad in it!" The Rev. Jean Darnall, who with her husband Elmer has been used greatly by God in nations around the world for over sixty years, says that she welcomes the new day by "greeting" God—Father, Son and Holy Spirit—reaffirming her love for Him and committing herself anew to honoring Him and fulfilling His will for that new day.

As a Christian I welcome each new day as a day of new beginnings. Sorrows and sadness are always old, but the joy of each particular day is always new. I must learn to leave behind the past with its sins and wounds. I do so by repenting of my sins and receiving forgiveness. My sins are then permanently removed. I then can welcome this new day with anticipation and excitement, receiving in faith healing for my many wounds, through the blood of Jesus. I can ask God, "What is Your plan for me for this particular day?" (as Father Archer Torrey always did during the early morning hours at Jesus Abbey in Korea), knowing full well that He will reveal it to me!

God Awakens My Ear To Hear.

Not only does God awaken me; He even awakens my ear, so that I can "listen as a disciple!" (Isaiah 50:4) Why would God awaken my ear? Because He who created me to hear and respond to His voice and so attain dignity as a full human being, desires to speak to me! God speaks in many and varied ways. He speaks to me as I read the Scriptures or hear them read, as I study or listen to another expound those powerful texts. But God chooses *to speak to me directly and personally,* as a friend speaks to a friend, in this waking hour. No other time could be so precious, so crucial to our life of discipleship than this time when the Lord awakens me and opens my ear to hear and be taught in intimacy by His Spirit. This is the time when the Spirit teaches me directly about the things of God, the hour when Jesus Himself disciples me so that I may walk faithfully before His Father, and my Father, in heaven.

This is the hour of meditation. Not the *only* hour to medi- tate, for my desire is to walk with the Lord so closely that I commune with Him continually throughout the day. Some meditators may prefer the late night hour of calm stillness, the late night watches, to ask God to speak to them person- ally. Others cannot escape the urgency of the beginning hour of each day when God Himself awakens them from sleep and opens their ears to hear "as those who are taught." God is ever-present, and He is eager to meet us at any hour of the day, with a personal word for that day. He daily gives us the word that He has prepared for each of us for that day. This is the time to meditate verse-by-verse, line-by-line, word- by-word, on the Bible. For this is where He speaks most clearly and most intimately. Indeed this is the time when the Holy Spirit gives me *understanding* of the deep truths of the Gospel, not in an academic way but rather in a deeply personal way. I discover that what the Scripture says is true: " . . . He awakens my ear to hear as those *who are taught!"* (Isaiah 50:4b) For is it not true that I understand the truth of God only as I *experience* that truth in the depths of my being?

The time of meditation is not the time to rely on another's prepared devotional booklet or on a Bible study guide. Nor is this the time for "spiritual reading" of the great Christian classics. No, this is the time to open my Bible and meet God face to face. This is the decisive time that determines the quality of my daily walk with the Lord. I simply have to ask,

"Lord, what is the Word You wish to share with me today? Speak, Lord, Your servant is listening."

The Spirit Plants God's Word In Me As I Listen.

How must I listen? I listen as a disciple, a learner and follower of my Master, as one who is passionately in love with Jesus and committed to following Him wholeheartedly. Who would doubt that God would speak as we approach Him in this way? He is the One who desires to commune and converse with us. He is the one who awakens us each morning that He might speak to us.

What is the Spirit of God doing as we listen? Dorothy Sayers sheds much light on the understanding of the Holy Spirit, as she does on the Trinity, in her book *The Mind of the Maker*. She relates the Trinity to the writing of a book and says every work of creation requires three things: a creative vision, the realization of that vision and the impact of that vision on others. This is somewhat "coded" language for the Trinity: God the Father is the "creative vision." Jesus the Son is the realization or revelation of the Father's vision; He is the *unique* Word of God. And the Spirit is the One who causes that vision to make an impact on people.[2]

The Holy Spirit is the one who unfolds the mysteries of God's Word and communicates that Word to us, causing us to be transformed. Only the Spirit can cause the Word that the Father speaks to our listening ears to actually penetrate our very being. The Word of God comes from Spirit to spirit, from God's Spirit to our human spirit. The Holy Spirit actually *plants* the Word into our human spirit.

But this does not happen automatically. For a seed planted in the ground to grow, we must consider many factors, such as the condition of the soil, the best time to plant, the amount of sunlight needed for it to grow, the necessity of water, and other factors necessary to produce fruit. In the same way, the meditator must prepare the soil of his heart to receive the seed of the Word, taking into account the need to be receptive, free from unconfessed sin, ready to nourish the seed that is to be planted. Only as the the meditator listens with a whole heart, welcomes with joy the words that the Bridegroom speaks, and is filled with a deep longing for those words to abide in him, only then does the Word of God become implanted in him. The meditating Christian must strive to be more open and sensitive to the Spirit and to enter into deeper fellowship with Him. For this implanting takes place not as an objective, academic exercise, but as a deeply subjective, intimate engagement with the Spirit.

The implanted Word Enables Me to Sustain the Weary.

When God opens my ear to "hear as those who are taught," He then gives me the "tongue of a teacher."[3] His purpose is to equip me to "sustain with a word him who is weary." Who are the weary ones of the world today? Many are those who are tired and exhausted from physical labor and oppression, and surely they would be included here. Innumerable also are those who are weary from emotional pain and mental anguish. Most certainly the Lord wants His people to sustain these people as well. But most likely the "weary" ones of whom Isaiah speaks are those who have suffered anguish and guilt because of their own sin, and their inability, or refusal, to seek God in their misery. The Lord Himself cries out to His people to comfort the weary ones, imprisoned in themselves: "Comfort, comfort My people, says your God. Speak tenderly to Jerusalem, and cry to her that her warfare is ended!" (Isaiah 40:1-2)

Hundreds of years later, Jesus spoke to the great crowds of people who were harassed and helpless, like sheep without a shepherd—people who, rather than being freed from their spiritual burdens, were instead heavy laden with the demands and controls of empty religious ritual. His invitation was, "Come to Me, all who labor and are heavy laden, and I will give you rest." (Matthew 11:28) What power lies in His simple invitation! The promise of rest can be found only in the Creator of all things! Today these weary ones are the billions of people who seek God but cannot find Him, entrapped by human systems of deceit and destruction, comprising more than one half of the world's population! A weary one may live in some remote corner of the world, or perhaps he could be your neighbor across the street.

"The Lord God has given me the tongue of those who are taught, that I may know how to sustain with a word him who is weary." God awakens me each morning, awakens my ear to hear His Word to me for that day, so that I may become equipped to bring His message of rest to a restless world. Yet so often we make tired people even wearier when we speak to them, rather than giving them rest. One of the strongest criticisms of the Church today is that the weary sinner cannot find rest in our midst. How could this be?

Could it be that God's Word does not dwell deeply within our own spirits, that we are not truly abiding in His Word but merely giving intellectual assent to it? Are we more interested in performing great works and sponsoring events for the Lord than in sitting at His feet and learning from Him? Are we, without having listened to God, merely speaking human wisdom and knowledge that brings more weariness rather than rest? Could it be that we as the Church of the living God are busy trying to *know about God* but failing to *know Him?*

If we are to be God's voice of rest and life to a weary, sin-sick world, our most important priority must be to meet God each morning in the sanctuary of our souls and eagerly wait to hear Him speak His Word, not to the world in general but to us personally! God's Spirit then will begin to renew our minds so that we are transformed into life-giving agents of God's love for the world.

I Must Obey the Word Implanted By the Spirit.

Just as important as listening, and hearing God when He speaks, is obeying what He says to us. The Word of God does its work in us when we obey. Jesus, the true Suffering Servant, responded to His Father's speaking to Him by obeying with joy all that the Father spoke to Him. His words in Isaiah 50 are our words as well: "The Lord God has opened my ear, and I was not rebellious; I turned not backward." (Isaiah 50:5) We are blessed to be God's servants, and our prayer is always that of young Samuel: "Speak, Lord, for your servant hears." My ear is that of a listener, and my greatest joy is to actually do what my Lord tells me to do.

The remainder of this Song of the Suffering Servant promises God's care and vindication for the meditator who listens and obeys. The Lord Himself becomes my Vindicator. He gives me a "face like a flint"—single-minded, undistracted in the face of all opposition or even persecution, determined to do His will.

Listening and Obeying: A Key to Spiritual Formation

Our desire is for Christ to be re-formed within us, so that our character may be remolded to conform to His character, our love and devotion to the Father modeled after His own. This in fact is one of the key works of the Holy Spirit in the life of the believer. As He works in us to cause us to conform to the image of Christ He uses the Word of God as His tool. Our response to that Word must be one of *listening* and *obeying*.

The Blessings of Obedience

The Apostle James, in his epistle, continually emphasizes the importance not only of hearing the Word of God but also of living in practical obedience to that Word. If we only hear the Word we will forget it, but the "doer who acts, he will be blessed in his doing." (James 1:25) In hearing and obeying we find release, joy and fruitfulness.

The year 1979 marked an important milepost in Ellen's and my life and ministry. We faced a crucial decision regarding the future strategy of our work as missionaries. Actually, the decision was whether to obey or not obey what God already had spoken to us through His Word as well as in times of prayer.

Our decision involved leaving one position and going to another. We had been missionaries for over eighteen years with one mission organization. We loved this organization, especially the friends and co-workers with whom we served. Our financial needs were amply provided for with a substantial salary, insurance, health and retirement benefits as well as provision for educational experiences for our three children, who at the time were in high school, middle school and elementary school. God was blessing our ministry, and we were reluctant to leave.

At issue was the training and commissioning of young Korean Christians to go as missionaries to the world. Because our ministry was with young people, especially university students, we faced the conflict and tension of being well-subsidized missionaries with relatively few financial worries, while the young people we would commission would have no such benefits and few resources. We concluded that we could more effectively train and send them as missionaries if we related more closely to them not only spiritually but also economically. Over a period of many months the Lord had been speaking to us and directing us to become a part of another mission organization which would enable us to more effectively carry out these goals. The problem was that this organization provided no financial benefits, no provision for our children's education, no health insurance.

Ellen and I both knew that the only way to come to a decision would be for each of us, separately and then together, to listen to the Lord in our times of morning meditation on the Word of God and then to obey whatever He said. We did not meditate in order to receive an answer to our prayer. No, that would be prayer but not meditation. We meditated each day simply to meet God, to behold His wondrous face, and to hear anything He had to say to us that day. And He did indeed meet us, and spoke to us both, separately at first, and showed us clearly that we were to make this important change.

I remember the day very clearly, when the Lord told us to step out in faith and follow Him, leaving one mission organization and going to another. It was September 24, 1979. I remember because of the way God spoke to us.

When we finally decided that if we were to obey God we must obey Him fully, whatever the cost, and when we prayed that prayer of commitment to Him, on that very day God brought to mind a Scripture passage: Haggai 2:18-19. Although I was familiar with the content of the prophecy of Haggai, I did not immediately remember the content of these particular verses before I read them again. So we opened our Bibles and began to read:

> *Consider from this day onward, from the twenty-fourth day of the ninth month. Since the day that the foundation of the Lord's temple was laid, consider: Is the seed yet in the barn? Indeed, the vine, the fig tree, the pomegranate, and the olive tree have yielded*

*nothing. But from this day on I will bless
you!*

" . . . From the twenty-fourth day of the ninth month!"
This was the very day we made the decision to obey the Lord
fully! Of course, the ancient Hebrew calendar is different
from the calendar we moderns use. But for us, it *was* on the
twenty-fourth day of the ninth month of our calendar that
God spoke these very words to us. How faithful the Lord is
to confirm His Word to us, sometimes in dramatic ways such
as this! We usually do not receive such miraculous guidance
as this, but this was a time of crisis, when we had to make
a life-changing decision. And this is the way the Lord chose
to respond.

Truly since that day, September 24, 1979, the Lord has
been faithful to His Word. He was always faithful, long
before that day; but since that day of deciding to obey Him
without reservation, we have been more fully aware of how
the Lord has granted His enabling and empowerment, His
provision far beyond all expectations, and His fruitfulness
in ministry. Yet we realize that this is not because of us, not
even because of our obedience. It is only because of God's
faithfulness. All fruit comes from Him, and He is faithful to
use all His servants in ways that will glorify Him and will
produce the maximum fruit for His Kingdom.

God simply wants our complete obedience. The meditator on the Word of God is one who hears and obeys, so that
Christ may be formed in us and we may be useful to God
as His servants. At times we must walk through valleys or
situations when we cannot see clearly where we are going.
We make mistakes and seemingly have to start all over
again. Only Jesus is perfect in hearing and obeying. But we
Christians are becoming like Him, being molded daily into
His image.

Is not our heart's deepest desire to continue to learn from our Master, who sought every opportunity throughout each day to draw close to His Father, to hear His word and then to do His Father's will? Our life is a walk with God. Our desire is to walk with Him so closely that we can hear Him, even when He whispers; and to walk with Him in such devotion that we are ready to obey whatever He says. This is the way the Early Church believers lived, and they turned the world upside down! Why not respond to Him now to become that meditator in whom the Spirit plants the seed of the Word of God, and whom God will use then to transform the world?

Invitation to the Banquet Table
Personal Meditation on Psalm 139

1. Review the four simple steps of meditation:
First, prepare your heart.
Second, listen to all God wants to say to you through the text.
Third, seek to meet God as He reveals Himself to you.
Fourth, respond to Him in prayer and obedience.

2. Read through the entire chapter of Psalm 139.
Open yourself to God and listen as you read.
Try to understand what the psalmist wants to express through this psalm.

3. Meditate on Psalm 139, **verse 6.**
Such knowledge is too wonderful for me.
It is high; I cannot attain it.
Consider the greatness of God and His knowledge of you.
Tell God that you would like to know Him more deeply.
Ask Him to continue to share with you His knowledge of you.
Listen to what the Lord wants to say to you personally!

4. Write down in your Meditation Journal what the Lord
says to you.
Or you may write out your prayer to Him.
Allow the Spirit to lead you as you listen to the Lord.

5. Take time now to *wait upon the Lord.*
Give Him your heart. Ask Him to reveal Himself to you.

6. Spend time in prayer.
Thank God for His word to you.
Commit yourself to obey Him.

Chapter Seven

The Faith-Awakening Word

"I followed the Lord my God whole-heartedly . . ."
Joshua 14:8 (NIV)

Caleb was one of the great pioneers of faith who trusted God and was willing to follow Him completely in the face of seeming disaster. The accounts of Caleb found in Joshua fourteen and Numbers thirteen and fourteen tell us that he was a man of undoubting faith and also an enduring pioneer for the Lord even at the age of eighty-five! But it tells us more. It tells us that behind Caleb the man of faith, the pioneer, was a Caleb we must know before we can understand his dynamic conquests: Caleb the meditator!

The biblical account in Joshua takes place after Israel has made the initial conquest of the land of Canaan. The Israelites now reside in the Promised Land, and Joshua is delegating to the various tribes the land that still must be conquered. "So now give me this hill country," cried Caleb, " . . . for you heard on that day that the Anakim were there, with great fortified cities. It may be that the Lord will be with me, and I shall drive them out just as the Lord said!"[1]

The Cry of Missions

Is this not the cry of missions? "Give me this hill country, this land, this nation?" Of course we must remember that Caleb was not on a missionary journey but rather engaged in military conquest. His sole purpose was to defeat the inhabitants of Hebron and drive them out in order to inhabit their land. Yet we must remember also that God had promised this land to Israel in order to fulfill His promise to Abraham that all the nations of the world would be blessed in him. (Genesis 12:1-3) In this formative period of Israel's history, military conquest was the way Israel came into the position of being able to bless the nations.

Today we do not engage in military warfare to advance the cause of world evangelization. Rather, servanthood is the true mark of our mission to the world. In this greater sense, when we say, "Lord, give me this land, this hill country, this people group, that I might go and serve them so that they can come into Your Kingdom," then we can use this cry of Caleb as a "missionary cry." This was the cry which the Father put upon the lips of His Son, Jesus, with that great invitation, "Ask of Me, and I will make the nations your heritage, and the ends of the earth your possession." (Psalm 2:8) And it is the cry the Father permits *all* His sons and daughters to make to Him, as joint heirs with Christ, His only begotten Son.

God has invited us to become coworkers with His Son for the evangelization of the world, and we must continue to intercede for the salvation of those nations, particularly the unreached nations of the world. If you have never done so, why not ask the Lord now to place a nation, or a people group, on your heart so that you can continue to cry out to Him on behalf of those people?

The Land Caleb Sought

What was the land like that Caleb sought? It was Hebron, a land of giant warriors (Anakim), with great, fortified cities! A people who could not be defeated, a land that was impossible for most other nations to even consider invading. Yet this was the people God had placed on his heart, and Caleb was undaunted by circumstances, wholly committed to pursuing his goal.

"It may be that the Lord will be with me . . . and I shall drive them out!" Here we see Caleb the man of faith, ready to trust God to do the impossible. Just as Sarah and Abraham had done before him, Caleb trusted the Lord who had promised, because he knew that He was faithful. All Caleb needed was the *presence of the Lord!* Nothing else would suffice. His predecessor Moses had insisted on this one thing before leading God's people into the wilderness past Mt. Sinai. Moses cried out to the Lord: "If your presence will not go with me, do not bring us up from here . . . for is it not in Your going with us that we are distinct, I and Your people, from every other people on the face of the earth?" (Exodus 33:14-16)

The presence of the Lord is the fount of every blessing, the source of every good thing that comes from God! After Jesus gave the Great Commission to His disciples, He blessed them with this same blessing: "Behold, I am with you always, to the end of the age!" (Matthew 28:20) And this same confidence in the Lord's abiding presence was the foundation of Caleb's faith.

"This hill country of which the Lord spoke . . ."

But we must know more about Caleb's passion. What was the source of this desire? Was it Caleb himself? Or was it God? Caleb reminded Joshua that this was the land of which *"the Lord spoke on that day!"* So this was more than a human desire, this passion Caleb had in pursuing the conquest of this land. When, then, did the Lord speak to Caleb about this land? Forty-five years before, when the twelve spies first began to spy out the land before the original conquest! Caleb, now eighty-five years old, was only forty when the Lord first spoke to him about Hebron!

Is this not the heart of missions? God speaks to us about a people, or a nation or an area of the world. We listen and then embrace God's Word in our hearts and begin to pray for those people, while God by His Spirit plants them deeply within our hearts. We study and do research about them, perhaps even visit them, and we can never forget them. They will never fade away, because God Himself has placed them in our hearts. We continue to hold on to the Word, believing, trusting, ready to obey. This "planting of the Lord" becomes the seed of missions, the beginning of a lifelong commitment to intercession for that nation, or of actually going to that nation as a missionary or financially supporting others who go. We discover that the same Spirit that entered Caleb has indeed come upon us as we seek to obey God in the world!

"I brought Him word . . . as it was in my heart."

"I brought him word again as it was in my heart," Caleb told the people of Israel as he recounted the spy trip. (Joshua 14:7) Some translations read, "I brought him a faithful word." Others simply say, "I brought him what was in my heart." But what does it mean to be faithful? Jeremiah, speaking against the false prophets who have no word from the Lord but only their own dreams, counters by saying, "Let the prophet who has a dream tell the dream, but let *him who has my word speak my word faithfully!"* (Jeremiah 23:28) To be faithful to the Lord we must first have a Word from the

Lord to which we can be faithful. Whatever may be the accurate translation, obviously Caleb had received a Word from the Lord. He had a Word in his heart. So we must ask, what were the conditions under which Caleb received the Word that was in his heart, which enabled him to give a faithful report to Moses?

How the Twelve Spies Entered the Land

All of the twelve spies were strong leaders, every one of them a chief from one of the tribes of Israel. Not one of them lacked faith or courage. All were aware that God already had promised to give the land of Canaan into the hands of Israel, and all had much experience in warfare. Yet we are told that the great majority, ten of the twelve, lost all their courage and reacted with fear and complete disbelief. How did this come to pass?

Imagine that you are there as a reporter, watching these twelve valiant men begin to enter the Promised Land. Most of them, in fact ten of them, did not even hesitate as they crossed over the boundary into the new land. They knew what they were doing and were confident of their strength and ability. Quickly they discovered how valuable the land was, how abundant its fruit. But they also discovered something else. The cities were much larger than they had imagined, and the people living there were much stronger than they had thought. And then there were the Anakim, the giants! They were filled with fear and saw nothing but impossibility.

As you are observing the other two spies, however, you notice that they do not enter the new land quite the same way as the majority of the spies. These two enter with the eyes of faith and with prayerful hearts. As they approach the border crossing, they pause and listen. They listen carefully to all that God wants to say to them about the land. They desire to see what God sees, and what He wants them to see.

This small difference, easily missed by a casual observer, made the all the difference in the way the spies reacted inside the land. All saw the same thing, all must have experienced shock and fear, and all understood that the human odds were against their being able to conquer the land. Yet ten spies returned with a negative report, two with a positive one. History would have been turned back that day had the majority had their way, but instead new history was created, all because these two men, Caleb and Joshua, *listened to the Lord before they entered the land!* This is why Caleb could later say, "I brought him word again that was in my heart!" God spoke to Caleb; His Holy Spirit then planted that word deeply within Caleb's inner person, so that the Word took root and produced the fruit of obedience.

God's Word Never Remains In the Past Tense.

God's Word is never just past tense. None who heard God speak in ancient times could ever contain that whole Word or claim it only for themselves. The Word is dynamic, not static. It is intended for, and sufficient for, all ages and all peoples. Every Word God spoke in Holy Scripture is spoken to everyone, in every place, "all with equal directness; no one is disadvantaged by distance in space or time."[2]

Meditators on God's Word are quick to realize that the Word of God is never like a finished painting, to be surveyed or studied as an historical document. The Bible is complete, and it is inspired in its final form. But it continues to be new each moment. Each time of meditating even on the same passage of Scripture is totally different from the last, because God is speaking in different ways, emphasizing different aspects of His truth each time I listen. Each time I meditate on the Gospel of John, for example, it is so completely new that it is as if I had never read it before!

St. Augustine taught us that it is not sufficient to depend on previously received insight or to simply know the testimonies of God. Rather, we must "continually receive and be *inebriated* by the fountain of eternal light!"[3] Perhaps this was the sin of the ten spies. They had received the Word from the Lord in the past. They knew that He had promised to give them the land as their inheritance. But they were acting on stored up knowledge of God's Word, rather than meeting God each moment, existentially, in His Word. They knew the testimonies of the Lord, but refused to allow those testimonies, that Word from the Lord, to overwhelm them and continually fill them with awe and wonder at the God who not only parted the Red Sea once in Israel's history but who continues to part all the seas and remove all the barriers that lie before His people who are walking in faithful obedience. The Word of God did not meet with faith in the lives of these ten spies. It remained with them as truth and as a testimony, but it did not change their lives. All they had to depend upon, then, as they entered the land, was their own self-confidence.

Listening As a Meditator

Caleb listened as a meditator. Was he anxious to receive a "new Word from the Lord?" No, he already had the Word from the Lord, spoken in the wilderness of Paran, well before he began his journey with Joshua. He did not need a new Word, just as today's meditator does not seek only a new Word from the Lord each time he meditates. The old Word is sufficient, it only needs to be spoken with new freshness by the Lord Himself, directly to me, penetrating my life and thought, restoring my emotions, giving firm direction to my will so that I may walk according to that Word.

Caleb did not ask God for a new Word that day, concerning the land of Canaan. He must have asked Him simply, "Lord,

I have heard you speak, and I trust in You and the Word that You already have spoken. Would you like to speak to me further as I prepare to enter this land to spy it out? Is there anything I need to know to fulfill the work You have given me to do?" And this is the way meditators today "enter the land," or begin a new day, or venture into a new mission or ministry for the Lord.

How wonderful it would be if Scripture recorded all the details of the conversation Caleb and the Lord must have had that day. Yet that was the Lord's personal word to Caleb, and we do not need to know. Surely the Lord must have spoken to Caleb and thanked him for trusting Him and committing himself to be faithful to His Word. The Lord also must have reassured him of His promise, perhaps warning him of the dangers to expect. But above all the Lord must have comforted Caleb and encouraged him to proceed in faith. Isaiah may have captured the essence of what the Lord spoke to Caleb that day, for Isaiah also was a listener, a meditator. "Fear not, for I am with you; be not dismayed, for I am your God; I will strengthen you, I will help you; I will uphold you with my righteous right hand!" (Isaiah 41:10)

Caleb returned and gave an honest and faithful report to Moses. He simply spoke to Moses the *Word that was in his heart!* "I followed the Lord my God whole-heartedly," spoke Caleb. Moses agreed and said, "The land on which your feet have walked will be your inheritance and that of your children forever, because you have followed the Lord my God whole-heartedly." (Joshua 14:7-9 NIV)

Becoming a Pioneer of Faith

Pioneers of faith are not born that way. Faith does not simply arise because someone has a desire to live by faith, or even because one makes a decision to live by faith. No, faith comes from hearing the Word of God! Only those who meet

Jesus afresh each day, gazing into His wondrous glory and listening attentively with the "ear of a disciple," will become men and women of faith. How desperately we need young pioneers of faith in this new age! But they must become *meditators* before God will call them to be His pioneers, because only those who hear from God on a regular basis can begin new work for God.

Caleb indeed was such a man. It is crucial to remind ourselves again of how he became one of the greatest pioneers for God. He *continually listened* to the Lord, always ready to hear Him speak, even it was only a word of encouragement. Here is the process: Caleb listened to the Lord. The Lord spoke to Caleb. And the Spirit of the Lord *planted that word* in the heart of Caleb, so that the word would never leave him but would instead bear much fruit. The implanted word transformed Caleb into a pioneer of faith. His commitment to the Lord was whole-hearted. Listening and obeying—two essential keys to the victorious life! The Spirit of the Lord will do the rest.

Dangers of a Leader Not Abiding In the Word of God

But what about those ten spies, the majority, who did not continue to listen to God, who chose to depend on themselves rather than abiding in God's ongoing Word to them? The biblical record stands: Their negative report caused resentment and rebellion among the whole nation of Israel, and they all died by a plague sent by the Lord Himself! (Numbers 14:37-38) Caleb and Joshua were the only two of all the "men of fighting age" who left Egypt, to actually enter into the Promised Land.

Today also there is a grave danger facing the Church, and that is the danger of leaders who lead out of their own wisdom and knowledge because they do not abide in the

Word of God. The dangers we face today are the same as those faced by Israel in Caleb's day. They are as follows:

1. Fear of Man

The first danger is the fear of man. This describes the person who is over-impressed with people and under-impressed with God, one who is more concerned about what people think about him than about what God thinks. Only the Word of God will deliver us from the fear of man into the only fear God wants, which is the fear of the Lord!

2. Low Self-Worth

Fear of man leads to low self-worth, having no sense of one's true value as a person. The ten spies despised themselves to the extent that they saw no dignity in themselves. "There we saw the Nephilim . . . and we seemed to ourselves like grasshoppers, and so we seemed to them!" (Numbers 13:33) The ten spies spoke it but did not understand the principle that how we see ourselves determines how others see us. If we see ourselves as worthless, others see us in the same way. But the meditator understands who he is in God and therefore has great dignity because he abides in the Word of God.

3. Subjectivity

Whose gospel were the ten spies proclaiming? Certainly not God's! They had never even listened! Perhaps they were proclaiming the "gospel of human reason," for they knew clearly that it was obviously impossible to defeat such a foe. The leader who does not abide in the Word of God will preach a subjective gospel! But the world does not long to hear such a gospel—the gospel of a certain denomination, or of a mission society, and certainly not of any single individual. Only if God speaks to me and I listen, on a regular basis, do I have a message for the world.

4. Diversion from God's Plan

The leader who does not abide in the Word of God is highly subject to diversions, easily sidetracked by less important things. Such a leader may have much vision, indeed too much human vision—vision of the flesh; and such vision will lead his people astray rather than into the presence of the Lord. How strange that this kind of leader often takes such pride in his own ideas while neglecting God's!

5. Limited Ministry

The result is that this leader's ministry, and the ministry of the group he may be leading, will be severely limited. Because where there is no abiding in God and in His Word, there is no vision at all. Consequently he is limited by his lack of knowledge of God and of His will, and this leads to boredom and monotony among his people.

6. Generating Complaint

The people of Israel were disillusioned by the majority report and predictably lost all hope. Those who lose hope due to unrealized expectations, especially if leaders cause this loss, will complain and begin to talk negatively. All that is left is what was left of the nation of Israel: a crowd of complainers and gossipers.

7. Inciting Rebellion

But the greatest danger of all that comes from a leader who does not abide in God's Word, is that there inevitably will arise dissent and rebellion among those he serves. Indeed, the rabble-rousers of Israel actually attempted a coup d'etat. They were beginning to choose a new leader to replace Moses, one who would take them back to Egypt! But they were unable to do so, because Moses was an intercessor! A man of the Word! A man of prayer! [4]

Meditation on God's Word—focusing our lives on Jesus, the Word of God, filling our minds and hearts with His words, walking in the presence of the Lord with a listening and obedient ear, always ready to hear and always ready to obey—this is the life that is pleasing to God, and the life God will use for His glory.

A Man Who Followed the Lord With A Whole Heart

Joshua paid the greatest tribute to Caleb when he said, "You have whole-heartedly followed the Lord my God." God asks for nothing else from a pioneer of faith. Now Caleb is eighty-five years old, still pioneering for the Lord!

Caleb gives thanks to God for "keeping him alive these forty-five years," and then makes this remarkable statement: "I am still as strong today as I was in the day that Moses sent me; my strength now is as my strength was then, for war and for going and coming!" (Joshua 14:11) What could he mean by such a radical statement? Paul gave the answer, many hundreds of years later, when he said, "So we do not lose heart. Though our outer nature is wasting away, our inner nature is being renewed day by day!" (2 Corinthians 4:16) Paul and Caleb, two great pioneers of faith who walked before us, give us the clue to a life filled with the excitement of knowing God. God's view of health, they both would say, is not that our physical bodies, when they grow old, retain the same physical strength as they had when we were younger. God indeed does care for the welfare of His servants and wants us to be in good physical health. He provides ways for us to maintain our bodies, and meditation accompanied by physical exercise is one of them.

But there is strength greater than physical strength. That strength is what will carry us through the many years of trials and hardships, even persecutions. That is the strength of the spirit, the strength of the soul—spiritual, mental, emotional strength, strength of will. No one could doubt that Caleb was a mighty man of God, a valiant warrior. Perhaps his physical strength was stronger than most men his age, but his real power lay in his daily walk with the Lord. Caleb attributed his good health and long life to the fact that he *"followed the Lord God whole-heartedly"* after the Spirit had planted God's Word in his heart.

Often when I teach young people to meditate, I challenge them to envision their lives in the middle to latter part of the 21st century. What will your life be like when you are 85 years old? Where will you be? What will you be doing for the Lord? Recently I was rewarded with a beautiful answer from a young man in the Charlotte, North Carolina, YWAM (Youth With A Mission) Discipleship Training School: "I will be in Hokkaido, Japan, where I will have lived for most of my life; perhaps a little bent over but standing straight in the Lord, continuing to listen to Him as He leads me in my mission work and trying to honor Him as my Japanese colleagues and I prepare teams of Japanese youth to go throughout the world teaching martial arts as they spread the Gospel of Jesus Christ."

God did not include the story of Caleb in the Bible just to encourage old people. No, it is especially for the young. As we begin our walk with the Lord, at whatever age we begin, we must learn from Caleb the secret of life-long fruitful ministry for the Lord. God guarantees the future of the meditator! We just keep walking with the Lord, listening to Him in His Word and obeying Him. And we will become fruit bearers!

Caleb's faith was a *living* faith, not just a faith of the past. As he recalled God's past deeds and continued to recommit himself to the present task, God continued to reawaken Caleb's faith and reconfirm His calling to be a world changer. Faith is a daily thing. It cannot be collected and stored, to be used at one's convenience. We must trust God every day in every instance, and we must listen to Him each step of the way. A pioneer of faith enjoys a special relationship with God, depending upon Him, listening to Him in every situation, especially in crucial times such as Caleb was entering. Are we not all called to be like Caleb?

Yes, there are others, many others, who walk the way of Caleb. Let us now see how the Holy Spirit planted God's word in the life of a young girl who would change the world, and in the lives of more modern pioneers of faith who have been used by God to change nations and open new areas for the Gospel.

Invitation to the Banquet Table
Personal Meditation on Psalm 139

1. Review the four simple steps of meditation:
First, prepare your heart.
Second, listen to all God wants to say to you through the text.
Third, seek to meet God as He reveals Himself to you.
Fourth, respond to Him in prayer and obedience.

2. Read through the entire chapter of Psalm 139.
Open yourself to God and listen as you read.
Try to understand what the psalmist wants to express through this psalm.

3. Meditate on Psalm 139, **verses 7 and 8.**
Where shall I go from your Spirit? Or where shall I flee from your presence?
If I ascend to heaven, you are there! If I make my bed in Sheol, you are there!
God continually pursues you until you allow yourself to be "captured" by Him in love.
Listen to what the Lord wants to say to you personally!

4. Write down in your Meditation Journal what the Lord
says to you.
Or you may write out your prayer to Him.
Allow the Spirit to lead you as you listen to the Lord.

5. Take time now to *wait upon the Lord.*
Give Him your heart. Ask Him to reveal Himself to you.

6. Spend time in prayer.
Thank God for His word to you.
Commit yourself to obey Him.

Chapter Eight

Receiving the Seed of God

"Receive . . . the implanted word."
James 1:21

"For the eyes of the Lord move to and fro throughout the earth that He may strongly support those whose heart is completely His." (2 Chronicles 16:9 NASB) The Spirit of God continually searches for those who focus their lives on God in deep devotion, so that He can in turn strengthen them in order to use them without reservation for His purposes in the world. He found such people in three remarkable meditators whose lives transformed the world.

Mary the Mother of Jesus

Mary was a humble country girl whose life was turned upside down by a visitation from the angel Gabriel. Although every Jewish girl's dream was to become the mother of the coming Messiah, Mary could hardly have expected it to happen to her in this way. Biblical scholars think that Mary was about thirteen years old, certainly no older than sixteen, when she was informed that she was to be the mother of our Lord. She was inexperienced in the world and not yet fully able to understand the full impact of the Word given to her. Yet her response to that Word reflected a deep inner maturity and an emotional stability far beyond her age.[1]

"The Holy Spirit will come upon you, and the power of the Most High will overshadow you; therefore the child to be born will be called holy—the Son of God," spoke the angel. (Luke 1:35) He was telling her that the Holy Spirit would *plant the seed* of Jesus, the Messiah, in her womb, and that she would bear the child without any human intervention. He assured her that nothing is impossible with God.

Mary's Submission To God

Perhaps you are among those who have wondered why Mary did not just run away, or why she did not simply go to her mother for advice. But Mary's answer is without a doubt one of the most beautiful confessions of faith found anywhere in the Scriptures. "Behold, I am the servant of the Lord; let it be to me according to your word." (Luke 1:38) If we knew nothing at all about Mary other than her total response of faith, we still would be forced to conclude that Mary is indeed the model for all who believe God with a trust and obedience that causes them to abandon all to the Lord, with no alternative but to follow Him.

How did she remain so serene and stable in the face of this supernatural manifestation from God? Obviously God had endowed her with a great longing for Himself, a deep desire to be immersed in the mysteries of God. She was ready, even at so young an age, to become God's channel for the salvation of the world. Ignacio Larranaga, who has produced one of the definitive works on the Virgin

Mary, says that with her "May it be done," she in fact "said 'Amen' to the night in Bethlehem, without a house, without a crib, without a midwife . . . 'Amen' to the flight into Egypt, unknown and hostile; 'Amen' to the hostility of the Sanhedrin; 'Amen' to the political, religious and military forces who had Jesus arrested; 'Amen' to the blood-bath of the crucifixion and death; 'Amen' to everything the Father arranged or permitted and she could not change."[2] By consenting to God's will, she was surrendering herself into the "all-powerful" and "all-loving" hands of our heavenly Father.

The Holy Seed

Mary was chosen by God to be the "womb of His Word," to receive the greatest gift of love that could ever be given, to conceive and give birth to Jesus, God's Word. Since that time, all generations have called her blessed.

The virgin conception and birth of Jesus Christ stands as the fundamental miracle of God's bodily entry into the world. Through this miracle God establishes clearly that the only Father of our Lord Jesus Christ is God Himself! Biological birth, tainted with the original sin of our ancestor Adam, is no longer the final answer. God's divine intervention through Mary points to the greater miracle of the Cross and Resurrection, where rebirth is made possible; sinful human beings can be reborn directly through the Spirit of God, and the bondage of their sin broken. Mary becomes a symbol of the *virgin Church*, the Church freed from sin. The prophet Hosea was the last to prophecy before Israel fell to Assyria (about 722 B.C.). At the time, Israel was nearly destroyed by her sin of rebellion against God. But Hosea prophesied about a coming new day, to be fulfilled ultimately in the Church, when God says that He will marry His *virgin People,* betrothing them to Him in faithfulness and righteousness. Mary's willingness to bear the Seed of God pleased God as He prepared the way for the emergence of His Bride, the Church.

"Womb of the Word"

After Jesus was born, the shepherds visited Mary and Joseph and the baby Jesus, and told the parents of the mysterious message of the angels. Later the Magi came to worship, and the elderly prophets Simeon and Anna both spoke concerning this child. All the people surrounding them who heard these messages were filled with awe and wonder. Mary and Joseph were unable to grasp the full meaning of the event, but Mary "treasured up all these things, pondering them in her heart." (Luke 2:8-19) Twelve years later, as the young boy Jesus discussed matters of the law with the teachers in the temple and then returned home with His parents and continued in subjection to them, Mary again "stored up all these things in her heart."[3]

Mary was a meditator, perhaps the greatest meditator among all the saints found in the Scriptures. Just as she allowed the Holy Spirit to plant the Holy Seed, Jesus, the Word, in her body at such a young, tender age, so she allowed the Spirit to plant the seed of the Word in her mind. She offered her womb to receive the Seed of God, Jesus the Word; but she also offered her mind and heart to be the "womb of the Word", the Word about Jesus. She embraced the Word, wrestled with it, pondered it, focused her whole being upon it and, most importantly, obeyed it.

Another evidence of Mary's meditation is her song, "The Magnificat," found in the first chapter of Luke's Gospel. This song is made up almost entirely of quotations from or allusions to Old Testament Scriptures, especially Hannah's prayer (1 Samuel 2:1-10) and the Psalms. At an early age,

Mary must have spent much time reading and meditating on the words of Moses and the prophets.

Mary's Years of Loneliness

Imagine Mary's years of loneliness as Jesus grew and matured into manhood. Some scholars believe that Joseph may have died sometime before Jesus began His ministry, since no mention is made of him again. Mary must have suffered from criticism about her early conception, and possibly had to endure misunderstanding and even abuse from others around her who did not comprehend what God was doing. She may have had to wrestle with her own doubts. And yet she always had the Word: the words of the shepherds, of the magi, the words of her own Son in the temple. They were planted deeply within her, and they gave her strength.

Mary At the Cross

The Bible does not tell us in detail how Mary's understanding of Jesus grew and developed. But is it not likely that about thirty years later, when Mary and the other women were weeping at the foot of the cross, that the Holy Spirit may have comforted Mary with the very words that she had stored in her heart like a treasure when Jesus was but a child?

Jesus told His disciples that His Spirit would guide them into all truth, and that He would bring to their remembrance all that Jesus Himself had taught them. Is it not probable, then, that the Spirit did this very thing for Mary as she knelt before the cross, comforting her troubled spirit and giving her a revelation of her Son, Jesus, which she had never had before?

Rewards of the Meditator

Such are the rewards of the meditator. At the cross, when the Holy Spirit comforted her with those words on which she had meditated many years earlier, Mary had great peace. She may have derived even more comfort and wisdom at that time than when she originally received them.

What encouragement and strength this brings to the believer! The words of Scripture before which I pause, on which I reflect and allow the Spirit to plant within me, will certainly comfort me this day, as I hear them. But an even greater blessing awaits the meditator! The Spirit who plants these words today will continually use them to enrich my life over the months and years to follow, and enrich others through me!

The First Christian Community

Jesus formed the first Christian community as He was dying on the cross. He committed Mary to His beloved disciple John, as his spiritual mother, and John to Mary, as her spiritual son—Mary the "great meditator" and John the "great lover!" This first community, formed around Mary and John, became the source of God's blessing to the world. Imagine the young community, by now growing larger, seated around the table at mealtime. John would ask Mary to share her intimate knowledge of Jesus as He was growing into a young boy and then a young man. Mary, in turn, would ask John to share some of his insights into the great love and compassion her Son Jesus showed to the multitudes. Such conversations went on every day at mealtime or at rest time. Surely Mary must have been an inspiration to John, on which he later drew as he wrote his five books of the New Testament: the Gospel of John; 1, 2, and 3 John; and The Revelation. John's writings take us deep into the love of God, as well as into the mysteries of God. Would it not be appropriate to remember that great meditator, Mary, and thank God for such a woman of God?

Mary—Total Abandonment

Henri Nouwen says that Mary responded to God with a "full 'Yes!'" She did not merely respond that one time before the angel Gabriel. No, hers was a "lifelong obedience to God's redemptive presence."[4] He adds that Mary's life was one of total abandonment to God's holy will, a complete emptying of herself in order to be filled with God's loving presence. And this is the goal of all meditators on the Word of God.

Mary is not only a model as a meditator; she is also a model Christian, who shows us the way God intended us to be as we respond to Him. Her complete obedience, her radical humility, and her "unwavering faithfulness"[5] all point the way to a meditator's lifestyle that will change the world.

George Mueller: The Implanted Word Produces Miracles.

We take a leap now through history to the 19th century, bypassing the many meditators of every age who changed the course of history by listening to God and obeying all that He spoke to them. Perhaps they will be subjects for another study, at another time.

If we were to examine the lives of the meditators throughout the history of the Church, we would discover that it is not the powerful people who produce fruit, work miracles and win victories for the Lord. Rather, it is the common man or woman of faith who believes in a mighty God, whom

God uses to display His glory. Certainly Mary was a prime example of this truth. And so was George Mueller.

George Mueller often said that we may meditate even though we are spiritually weak. Indeed we meditate because we are spiritually weak. We have no power in ourselves. We are not miracle workers. We are not healers. We are simply God's people who come before Him in His Word each morning with humility and meekness, submitting ourselves to that Word and asking God to work in our lives according to that Word.

Known by Christians today as the "father of the orphans," Mueller was known by his peers as a true man of meekness and humility. Because he submitted himself without reservation to God, he was able to sacrifice himself for the hundreds, later to become thousands, of orphans whom God committed to his care. God used this combination of submission and sacrifice, true meekness, or gentleness, to produce the miracles that we remember still today. Day by day, week after week, year after year, God miraculously provided food and sustenance for those orphans in Bristol, England, in the early 19th century.

Many have asked about the secret of George Mueller. How was he able to see such miracles take place on a regular basis, feeding and caring for the orphans with no strong financial backing from any human source? We should let George Muller answer for himself. To do so, it is important that we quote rather extensively from his brief autobiographical tract entitled *Soul Food*.

> *It has pleased the Lord to teach me a truth, the benefit of which I have not lost for fourteen years. I saw more clearly than ever that the first business to which I ought to attend every day, was to have my soul happy in the Lord. The first thing to be concerned about,*

was not how much I might serve the Lord, but how I might get my soul in a happy state, and how my inner man might be nourished.

I might seek truth to set it before the unconverted, I might seek to benefit believers, I might seek to relieve the distressed, and I might in other ways seek to behave myself as it becomes a child of God in this world, and yet, not being happy in the Lord, and not being strengthened in the inner man day by day, all this might not be attended to in the right spirit.

Before this time my practice had been to give myself to prayer after having dressed in the morning. Now I saw the most important thing I had to do was to give myself to the reading of the Word of God, and to meditate on it, that my heart might be comforted, encouraged, warned, reproved, instructed, and that thus, by means of the Word of God, my heart might be brought into experimental communion with the Lord.

I began therefore to meditate on the New Testament from the beginning, early in the morning. The first thing I did after having asked in a few words the Lord's blessing upon His Word, was to begin to meditate on the Word, searching, as it were, every verse to get a blessing out of it . . . not for the sake of public ministry, not preaching, but for obtaining food for my soul.

The result I found to be invariably this. After a few minutes my soul had been led to confession, or thanksgiving, or intercession, or supplication . . . it turned almost immedi-

ately into prayer. When thus I have been for a while making confession, or intercession, or supplication or having given thanks, I go to the next words of the verse, turning all as I go into prayer for myself or others, as the Word may lead to it, but still continually keeping before me that food for my own soul is the object of my meditation.

The difference, then, between my present practice and my former is this. Formerly, when I arose, I began to pray as soon as possible, and generally spent all my time till breakfast in prayer, or almost all the time. At all events I almost invariably began with prayer, except when I felt my soul to be more than usually barren, in which case I would read the Word. But what was the result? I often spent a quarter of an hour, or half an hour, or even an hour on my knees before having been conscious to myself of having derived comfort, encouragement, humbling of the soul, etc., and often after having suffered much from wandering thoughts, for up to half an hour, I only then began to really pray.

I scarcely ever suffer in this way now, for my heart being brought into experimental fellowship with God, I speak to my Father about the things He has brought to me in His precious Word.

It often astonishes me that I did not sooner see this point. And yet now, since God has taught me this point, it is as plain to me as anything, that the first thing the child of God has to do morning by morning is, to obtain food for his inner man.

> *Now, what is the food for the inner man?*
> *Not prayer, but the Word of God; and here*
> *again, not the simple reading of the Word of*
> *God, so that it only passes through our minds,*
> *just as water runs through a pipe, but consid-*
> *ering what we read, pondering over it, and*
> *applying it to our hearts.*
>
> *We may . . . profitably meditate, with*
> *God's blessing, though we are ever so weak*
> *spiritually; nay, the weaker we are, the more*
> *we need meditation for the strengthening of*
> *our inner man.*
>
> *How different, when the soul is refreshed*
> *and made happy early in the morning, from*
> *what it is when without spiritual preparation,*
> *the service, the trials, and the temptations of*
> *the day come upon one.*

George Mueller's own testimony speaks of the power of meditation. The Spirit of God implanted God's Word in his soul as he meditated. Even today he remains a witness to the changed life that comes from receiving the implanted Word in humility and meekness. When we meditate we open ourselves to God in the Word. We focus our whole attention on the words of the verse before us, asking Him to fill us with His Word that we might be living witnesses of the miracles wrought by that Word.

The Word Implanted In Lenna Belle

Joining the ranks of those meditators God has raised up in every century to be channels of His Word to bless the nations would be Lenna Belle. Lenna Belle Robinson is a modern day Caleb. They told her she was too old when she applied for missionary service. But she had always seen herself as a missionary. Even as a young medical doctor during America's Great Depression, she regarded her frugal, simple lifestyle as training for doing God's work, anywhere, under any conditions.

She retired from medical practice in Louisiana at the "new beginnings" age of sixty-one and set out for missionary work in Korea. But after a few years of doing short-term mission work in a large Christian hospital, they told her she was too old. The other missionaries, and the hospital where she worked, all let it be known that she might be better off going back home to rest from all her good labors, "seeing as how she was getting older now."

But Lenna Belle discovered through her treatment of patients that nothing was being done about epilepsy in the whole nation of Korea, even though treatment and drugs were available in the West that could control the disease and make normal living possible. With very little financial or moral support from anyone, she dared to attempt the impossible — she set out to completely control the disease in Korea.

How much my wife and I learned from Lenna Belle! Whenever we visited her home in the city of Incheon to encourage her we would always return thoroughly refreshed and inspired, renewed in our faith that God can indeed do anything and everything! We visited to encourage her, but it was she who did the encouraging! She would rise at four o'clock every morning to read through the Bible and meditate! She let us know that it was not old age that made her sleepless but it was God who woke her up early and awakened her ear to listen as a disciple. (Isaiah 50:4)

"This is the way I meditate," she told us repeatedly. "First I read through a passage of Scripture. You know, of course, that I'm always reading, I can never get enough of God's Word. I just want to read and read and read. But when I meditate," she said, "I meditate on just one verse of Scripture, possibly two verses if they are connected. You can *think about* a longer passage, but you can meditate best just by sitting before one verse. I simply ask the Lord if He has something He would like to say personally to me through this verse of Scripture. I listen, and then I obey." And that is Lenna Belle's way of meditating. Too simple, you might say? Simple indeed, but life changing!

After her time of meditation and prayer, and reading the Bible, she would spend all day, five days a week, traveling throughout the whole nation of Korea to minister to epileptic patients, even when she was in her seventies and eighties! She established "Rose Clubs"—small communities to counsel and treat patients with this feared, yet controllable disease—throughout the entire nation of South Korea! How deeply humble she was when she received the highest honor a civilian can receive from the Republic of Korea— the Presidential Order of Merit—giving all glory to God!

Yet Lenna Belle was still not satisfied. In her old age she began to develop a passion for ministering to the troubled youth of both Korea and America. She always wished she were younger, so that she could go directly to these young people to love them and show them God's great care and plan for their lives. She was grieved in her spirit as she carried the burden for these youth and she tried with all her might to challenge others to receive vision from the Lord to go out with the task of winning the youth for Christ. She was still doing this when she was in her late eighties!

Lenna Belle is one hundred and three years old now, having reluctantly agreed to cease her missionary activity in Korea at the age of ninety! But did somebody say she really is too old now? Was Caleb too old? You guessed it! Recently when we visited to encourage her, she completely overwhelmed us by her missionary zeal and her passion for the Lord and for His Word!

We never even had the chance to ask how she was doing. She was so busy sharing what God had spoken to her during her daily Bible meditation, and so busy showing us her twenty-five prayer notebooks (each three inches thick) in which she records her prayers for the seven hundred missionaries on her prayer list! She still gets up at four o'clock every morning because she says she works best before breakfast, meditating and praying for four hours before she begins her daily activities. She even finds time to read her favorite mystery novels in the midst of her busy schedule!

If you visit her, don't ever suggest that you think she is too old. She's just like Caleb, probably younger than you! And she's waiting for her next assignment from the Lord. She is "ruined for the ordinary," as Joy Dawson would say, because the Word of God is implanted deeply within her soul.

In this chapter we have met three meditators. All of them were weak and unable to do anything in their own strength. But the common bond that unites them is their willingness to submit themselves totally to the Lord, for whom nothing is impossible. They listened to the Lord, not just at set times but continuously throughout each day. But they not only listened, they were *doers* of the Word as well. And God used them to change nations.

His invitation still stands. You are invited to open yourself each day to God's Holy Spirit, so that He might plant the seed of God's Word in your inner person. That seed will grow and produce fruit in your life. And you also may become a nation-changer!

Invitation to the Banquet Table
Personal Meditation on Psalm 139

1. Review the four simple steps of meditation.
First, prepare your heart.
Second, listen to all God wants to say to you through the
text.
Third, seek to meet God as He reveals Himself to you.
Fourth, respond to Him in prayer and obedience.

2. Read through the entire chapter of Psalm 139.
Open yourself to God and listen as you read.
Try to understand what the psalmist wants to express
through this psalm.

3. Meditate on Psalm 139, **verse 9 and 10.**
*If I take the wings of the morning and dwell in the uttermost
parts of the sea,
Even there your hand shall lead me, and your right hand
shall hold me.*
Consider that God will continue to lead you regardless of
where you are.
His strong right hand will always uphold you.
Listen to what the Lord wants to say to you personally!

4. Write down in your Meditation Journal what the Lord
says to you.
Or you may write out your prayer to Him.
Allow the Spirit to lead you as you listen to the Lord.

5.Take time now to *wait upon the Lord*.
Give Him your heart. Ask Him to reveal Himself to you.

6. Spend time in prayer.
Thank God for His word to you.
Commit yourself to obey Him.

Part Three

The Power of The Word

God's Word is powerful
to make believers whole
and equip us for
ministry in the world.

God sends His Word
for many purposes:
To heal us
To restore us
To break and remold us
To feed us
To equip us.

This section will reveal to us how
meditating on the Word of
God allows these purposes
to be realized in
our lives.

Chapter Nine

The Healing Word

"He sent out His word and healed them . . . "
Psalm 107:20

She was an eighteen-year-old high school graduate in a large American city, ready to enter her freshman year at university. Instead, her long-standing addiction to drugs and alcohol caused her to enter a state psychiatric hospital as a patient. Hopeful at first, after prolonged treatment her doctor was forced to conclude that her illness was more severe than anyone had imagined. He reluctantly told her that this small room would very likely be her home for a longer period of time.

Some weeks later a group of women visited from a local Presbyterian church. One lady, carrying a large Bible, asked the head nurse if she could visit room by room and read the Bible to the mental patients. Despite a flat refusal, she persisted until finally the presiding physician overheard her earnest request and allowed her to read to his young patient. "But absolutely no witnessing or attempting to convert her," warned the psychiatrist, "just read the Bible. And no prayer."

So she read. She read to her one hour each day for two months, but her condition deteriorated and she seemed more like a vegetable, crouching unresponsively in a corner of her room, than a person. Yet the lady continued to read, one hour each day, choosing passages like the following:

For You formed my inward parts; You knitted me together in my mother's womb. I praise You, for I am fearfully and wonderfully made. Wonderful are Your works; my soul knows it very well. [1]

She would pause a moment to give time for the words to sink in. Then she would read another line from Jeremiah, "Before I formed you in the womb I knew you; before you came to birth I consecrated you."[2]

Another two months went slowly by with no improvement. Then, miraculously, in the next few months the young girl began to respond, listening and occasionally asking questions. By the end of six months she had completely recovered and was dismissed from the hospital, healed spiritually as well as emotionally. Today she is a strong, Spirit-filled Christian with a radiant faith.

She has no doubts about what happened. She knows that she was released and strengthened in her inner person, and healed by the Spirit of God. She had never been to a church. She had never before known the saving grace of Jesus Christ who was now her Lord. In fact no one in her family had been religious. But the Word of God was now implanted deep in her inner being through the Author of that Word, the Spirit of God Himself. God, through His Word, healed her from the inside out and transformed her into a beautiful woman of God.

He Sent Forth His Word and Healed Her.

What took place inside the life of this young woman to transform her so totally from a person who had no knowledge of God, enslaved to drugs and alcohol with no future outside the walls of her hospital room, into a beautiful, whole and healthy woman of God able to bear fruit for the Lord? We must turn to the psalmist for the answer, for she was one of those " . . . who sat in darkness and in the shadow of death, prisoners in affliction and in irons." (Psalm 107:10) But the psalmist extols God because "He brought them out of darkness and the shadow of death and burst their bonds apart . . . *He sent out His word and healed them,* and delivered them from their destruction." (Psalm 107:14,20)

The Lord who is "near to the brokenhearted and saves the crushed in spirit" *sent His word* and healed her! (Psalm 34:18) Jesus Christ, the eternal Word of God, came with compassion and healed her broken heart with the Word that was read to her by that faithful saint from the church in the city! God's Word did for her what she could not do for herself. The lady who visited her and read the Scriptures to her daily for six months was the "sower who went out to sow." The Holy Spirit used her obedience and compassion to plant the seed of God's Word in the young girl's heart and then caused the seed to take root and grow, producing the fruit that was now evident to all who saw her.

This young girl, this new meditator on God's Word, who now has become a "woman of the Word," perceived that she must have been "meditating sub-consciously" during her illness when the Scriptures were being read to her. She was not able to actively, consciously receive the Word, but that did not stop God's Holy Spirit from planting the Word in her!

This is the same Word of God that the writer to the Hebrew Christians describes as *"living and active, sharper than any two-edged sword."* (Hebrews 4:12a) The Word that originates from the heart of God with the power of His Spirit, the Word that brings wholeness and health to all who are burdened with hopelessness and despair, now came to dwell within her!

No one knew the power of this Word better than the Apostle Paul. So when he gave his farewell address to the elders of the Church of Ephesus, after warning them of the dangers that faced them both from outside and inside the Church, he concluded with these startling words: "And now I commend you to God and to the Word of His grace, which is able to build you up and to give you the inheritance among all those who are sanctified." (Acts 20:32) He did not commit the Word to them, because they were powerless. Instead, he committed them to the Word, because the Word of God is powerful and never fails. It is the Word of Christ, who "upholds the universe by the Word of His power!" (Hebrews 1:3b)

God's Word Always Succeeds.

God's Word never fails. It always succeeds in producing the results intended by God when He sends His word to a person or into a situation. Isaiah confirmed his absolute confidence in the Word when he declared, "For as the rain and the snow come down from heaven, and do not return there but water the earth, making it bring forth and sprout, giving seed to the sower and bread to the eater, so shall My word be that goes out from My mouth; it shall not return to Me empty, but it shall accomplish that which I purpose, and shall succeed in the thing for which I sent it." (Isaiah 55:10-11)

Students from Rutgers University, the State University of New Jersey, were concerned about the lack of a permanent Christian outreach ministry among the Korean-American students at Brown University and at the Rhode Island School of Design (RISD), both located in Providence, Rhode Island. Although there were Christian students at the two schools, there was no church or group strong enough to seek out non-believing students, witness to them and nurture them in Christian discipleship, forming in them a biblical Christian worldview.

As the Rutgers students were praying, they came across these words from Isaiah and were deeply impressed with the promise that God's Word would not return to Him empty without accomplishing the purpose for which He sent it. They began to meditate on these two verses asking God for enlightenment and guidance. God revealed to them that this was His Word of promise for the campus at Brown University. They held tightly to these verses as they prepared to have a "revival service" right on the campus of Brown.

They faced ridicule and lack of support even from some Christian students at Brown and RISD who doubted that a genuine move of the Holy Spirit could take place on the campus of such a prestigious Ivy League school. Besides, it was football Homecoming Week, and who would attend?

But God's Word does not return to Him void. The first night, Friday night before the big game and festivities, over seventy people attended the revival meetings. Saturday afternoon, the big Homecoming Day, saw that many people again, representing nearly a dozen ethnic and racial groups. And God moved in a mighty way through His Spirit.

Today there is a strong, vibrant and dynamic church on the campus of Brown University, with outstanding leaders who have a vision for the entire world. At least one reason for this church's existence is the small group of Rutgers University students who prayed and *meditated* on the Word of God, believing that God would do what He said He would do.

As they meditated they heard God speak, came to know His will and planned their strategy on the basis of the Word

God sent them. They listened to God and obeyed, opening the door for a mighty move of God on another university campus!

So it was with the young girl who was healed and able to leave the psychiatric hospital. She was healed because the Word of God, sent by God, performed the will of Her heavenly Father and did not return to Him void. Her presiding physician, a believer in the Jewish faith, understood what had happened. He, too, shared in her joy and confirmed her healing as having come directly from God. Indeed God sent His Word and healed her.

But her story does not stop there. She was able to enter college and became a good student with a strong, visible faith. As a born-again Christian, filled with His Holy Spirit, she continues to witness to others about God's faithfulness and power in Jesus Christ. Friends report that at times she goes to the university square, where many young people hang out. She never goes without carrying a large Bible, seeking out young people who are in situations very much like the one that she had been in, often asking them, "May I read the Bible to you?"

Three Things the Word of God Will Do

Jeremiah tells us that the Word of God will do three special things for us when the Holy Spirit plants that word inside us. God's Word is like a hammer, like fire and like wheat. (Jeremiah 23:28-29)

The Word of God is a *hammer* that breaks through the outer shell of resistance, rebellion and unbelief in our lives and lays open our inner hearts for God to touch. Once our hearts are open the Word becomes the *fire* of God to burn away all the chaff—the needless, wasteful and sometimes harmful attitudes and obstructions that cause destruction in our lives. Then the Word comes to us as *wheat*, to feed and nourish our souls.

Christians who continue to grow into maturity in the Lord are without exception those who seek God in His Word on a daily basis, meditating and feeding on that Word.[3] Just as baby birds wait longingly for their mother to come with food and then excitedly consume everything she brings, so the growing Christian longs for God's Word and receives it with boldness and confidence as God feeds and nourishes them and gives them growth.

God's Word performed His purpose for the young girl. She was totally transformed. For six months, daily hearing the Word of God read to her by a faithful servant of God enabled her to allow the Spirit of God to sow the Word deeply into her spirit.

The change did not happen overnight. Just as water, dripping slowly but steadily onto a rock will in time cause that rock to be totally reshaped, so the Word of God in time will reshape our spirits, our wills, our emotions, our thought life. Water is soft. A rock is hard. God's Word comes to us quietly, softly, slowly making its impact upon our hardened hearts. And change takes place. Meditation is the act of receiving that Word daily, allowing it to reshape our hardened hearts until God's will becomes our great delight.

Imagine what could happen in your life, as you read these words. This young girl did not know God. Neither she nor her family had attended a church. She was a patient in the psychiatric ward of a state hospital and even her own physician had given her up as being too difficult to help. Yet nothing is impossible with God. There are no problems He cannot solve, no disease He cannot heal, and no relationship He cannot renew.

If a person such as this can be so radically and totally transformed simply by hearing the Word of God read to her one hour a day for six months, what could happen in your life? You already love God; you seek to be filled with His Spirit and long for fellowship with Him. Imagine the transformation that will come to you as you begin to live in the Word, to abide in God's Word by listening to Him daily, seeking to meet Him as He reveals Himself through His Word!

Meditation is the first step that leads to the way of intimacy and deeper communion with God. Meditators realize that the Word of God is living and active, more alive than we are, able to work God's will within us in an unlimited way.

Meditation Is Used As a Tool In a Medical Practice.

Dr. Herbert Benson, a cardiologist and professor at Harvard Medical School, published an article in the *Harvard Business Review*[4] stating that meditation is a key factor in relieving stress in modern life. Later, in a lecture he reported that Harvard psychiatrists had found among their patients who were religious, significant emotional and physical responses that were a direct result of their meditating on single sentences or phrases from their scriptures! He even said that he urged patients to meditate once in the morning upon arising and once again in the evening before going to sleep. Of course this is precisely what King David prescribed in Psalm 1 where he tells us that the truly blessed person meditates on the Word of God *day and night!*

Many Christian doctors prescribe meditation on the Word of God during the recovery period for patients who have had mental or emotional illnesses, for those with serious physical illnesses that leave psychological scars and imprints on the patients, or for those who are being released from drug and alcohol dependency.

Reports from around the world tell of the power of Bible meditation in bringing healing and wholeness to God's people. Young men and women are overcoming withdrawal as they become freed from drugs and other addictions. People are being released from severe depression, anxiety or despair. Chronic sufferers of high blood pressure and extreme stress are discovering the "quiet center" where God speaks. God is at work today to heal His people. He continues to send His Word and heal.

God Continues to Send His Healing Word.

The closing decades of the twentieth century was a healing time for God's people. In contrast to the tragedies and atrocities of man's inhumanity to man, the Spirit of God moved powerfully throughout the world. Reports of healings and supernatural deliverances continued to flow in from the Suffering Church throughout those decades.

The Rev. Francis MacNutt visited South Korea often during the decade of the seventies to teach the Church about the healing ministry and to try to restore the ministry of healing to the Church. Hundreds of Protestant pastors and Catholic priests would gather for healing workshops in the mornings at the Jesuit's Sogang University, then meet with thousands of Christians and non-believers for healing rallies at indoor coliseums or sports stadiums in the evenings. I was present at many of those gatherings. One evening, in the city of Pusan, we experienced nearly every healing recorded in the New Testament, each one attested to by a Catholic priest or Protestant pastor who knew the person involved! What a mighty move of God's Spirit in response to the unity of His people! We could imagine God's heart as He was being honored by His people crossing denominational barriers to obey His command: "Behold, how good and pleasant it is when brothers dwell in unity . . . for there the Lord has commanded the blessing, life forevermore." (Psalm 133:1,3)

The morning after this great gathering, I was reading through the 108th Psalm before beginning a long drive to Seoul. I began to meditate on the first verse: "My heart is steadfast, O God! I will sing and make melody with all my being!" As I meditated God began to reveal His heart for His Church. He was pleased with the unity of His people and their willingness to dispense with long held prejudices between Catholic and Protestant Christians. God was honored because His Church was becoming steadfast. This was cause for great joy, a time to sing, a time to celebrate over the healing of God's Church.

I continued to meditate as I entered the expressway that would take me from Pusan to Seoul. And I began to experience a great joy and steadfastness in my own soul. This Scripture verse, only a few words in content, was lifting my soul into the very presence of God, and I began to sing and rejoice, making melody with all my being.

Suddenly God spoke to me and told me to take off my glasses, that He was healing my eyes! I had prayed for years for the healing of my eyes. Once I told my ophthalmologist, who was a devout Christian, that I wished God would heal my eyes. His reply was that "with your form of astigmatism, your miracle is that we can fit you with glasses!" During the years that I had been praying, God had revealed to me also that the healing of eyes involves much spiritual and emotional healing, so that we can begin to see Jesus who is constantly before us, and to see others through the eyes of Christ and not through our human eyes.

Now God was revealing to me that His healing of the Church, and His healing of my spiritual and emotional eyes, and His healing of my physical eyes were all part of the greater healing that He was bringing to the Korean Peninsula, and to me in particular.

I removed my glasses and continued the six-hour drive to Seoul without any hindrance. And I did not wear glasses again for seven years! Then, after seven years, I resumed wearing them again and still wear them today. But not because of astigmatism! No, God healed that, but for some reason known only to the Lord, He healed my astigmatism but only gave me temporary healing of my near-sightedness for the period of seven years! But the miracle was that although the Lord did not bring healing to my eyes during the long years that I had prayed earnestly for that healing, He did bring great healing to me during the thirty minutes I meditated on a single verse of Scripture! Indeed, God does send His Word to heal His people!

God is at work today to heal His Church. He continues to send His Word to heal and restore His people. Not all healing takes the form of physical restoration. Countless are the saints who through faith endure great suffering and even martyrdom. Many sincere Christians pray and meditate, fast and commit themselves to the Lord and still are not healed of their physical ailments. Certainly God heals them in deeper ways, in the depths of their souls and through His comforting presence with them. There are times when God's perfect healing is to take His loved ones home to be with Him eternally.

But this we know: Our Lord is the Lord who heals His people, who heals His Church, and who desires to heal the peoples of the world. Meditation prepares us to receive God's healing and to open ourselves to Him so that He may restore and equip us to be His healing community for a world in pain.

Invitation to the Banquet Table
Personal Meditation on Psalm 139

1. Review the four simple steps of meditation:
First, prepare your heart.
Second, listen to all God wants to say to you through the
text.
Third, seek to meet God as He reveals Himself to you.
Fourth, respond to Him in prayer and obedience.

2. Read through the entire chapter of Psalm 139.
Open yourself to God and listen as you read.
Try to understand what the psalmist wants to express
through this psalm.

3. Meditate on Psalm 139, **verses 11 and 12.**
*If I say, "Surely the darkness shall cover me, and the light
about me be night,"*
Even the darkness is not dark to you;
*The night is bright as the day, for darkness is as light with
you.*
Remember that God is present in any darkness you may
have to enter.
His light shines upon you even in your darkest hour.

You can walk through the valley, because Jesus is your
Leader.
Listen to what the Lord wants to say to you personally!

4. Write down in your Meditation Journal what the Lord
says to you.
Or you may write out your prayer to Him.
Allow the Spirit to lead you as you listen to the Lord.

5.Take time now to wait upon the Lord.
Give Him your heart. Ask Him to reveal Himself to you.

6. Spend time in prayer.
Thank God for His word to you.
Commit yourself to obey Him.

Chapter Ten

The Restoring Word

"He restores my soul."
Psalm 23:3

A deep tiredness was beginning to overwhelm me as our plane began the slow descent into Incheon International Airport near Seoul. Already twenty-two hours had passed since I left Boston to make the long trip over the North Pole to Korea. In spite of being in a jumbo jet traveling at speeds in excess of 500 miles per hour, I felt rather like a snail crawling slowly over the vast expanse of water and icy terrain. By the time I finally settled into my bed in Seoul I was wondering where I would get the energy to face the coming week's schedule of teaching eight hours a day and meeting all the people I wanted and needed to see during my brief visit to Korea. And all that would begin the very next morning!

What a surprise it was the next morning to feel refreshed and invigorated with new strength, rather than tired and lacking in energy. It all happened during my time of meditation. I had been meditating on 2 Corinthians, and that morning the verse to sit before and ask God to speak to me from, was, "For all the promises of God find their Yes in Him. That is why it is through Him that we utter our Amen to God for His glory." (2 Corinthians 1:20)

As I waited for the Lord with this verse before me, the Lord began to remind me of many of His promises: that those who wait upon the Lord will gain new strength, that in His presence is fullness of joy and steadfastness in spirit, soul and body. I thanked Him that all these promises have been perfectly fulfilled in Jesus Christ, and expressed to Him that my one desire was to see His face that morning and walk with Him throughout the day. As I waited I could sense His presence leading me into a new level of rest, for my body as well as for my soul. And I knew that I had been restored and was ready for all He had planned for the day and the week. As I concluded my time of meditation I shouted "Amen!" to the glory of God for His restoring me during those few minutes of meditating on His Word.

How true it is that God sends His Word to heal and restore His people! That same Word spoke to the young girl lying in the psychiatric ward of the big city hospital. We will call her Rhonda.[1] The Word came, she heard it and her spirit responded from deep within her. Rhonda was healed and restored, far beyond anyone's expectations, becoming a whole person in a way no one could have imagined.

The Word of God Will Restore Us.

How did the Word of God restore her? What took place within her inner being as she heard God's Word read and received that Word? What healing and restoration will happen in our lives as we become meditators?

Psalm 19 speaks of God's restoration of His people. The psalmist tells us that all of God's creation bears testimony to Him. The works of His hands—the mountains and seas, flowers and trees, clouds and sun—bear witness to His invisible attributes, His eternal power and divine nature, so much so that no human being is without excuse before God. (Psalm 19:1-5; Romans 1:20)

Who has not stood in awe before a magnificent sunset and seen the signature of the God who created it? Who could stand before the mighty, majestic sea and fail to have some sense of the Eternal Father, strong to save, who continues to come into our lives like the unceasing waves upon the shore? A simple rose, exquisite in its design and formation, speaks of its Maker and invites all who approach it to open themselves to the One who can produce a beauty in them that surpasses even the rose or the sunset.

God has placed an awareness of Himself—a "God-consciousness"—in every person, to which all nature and creation testify. Through it, the Spirit of God prepares each person to receive the Good News of the Gospel of Jesus Christ. God already had prepared Rhonda to receive His healing Word.

But the psalmist says more. While all creation testifies to God's existence and presence, it is the Word of God alone that bears witness to the finished, completed work of God in Jesus Christ for wholeness and salvation. The latter part of Psalm 19 describes the restoring work of God's word in our lives:

The law of the Lord is perfect, reviving the soul.
The testimony of the Lord is sure, making wise
the simple.
The precepts of the Lord are right, rejoicing the heart.
The commandment of the Lord is pure, enlightening
the eyes.
The fear of the Lord is clean, enduring forever.
The rules of the Lord are true, and righteous altogether.

More to be desired are they than gold, even much fine gold; sweeter also than honey and drippings of the honeycomb. Moreover, by them is your servant warned; in keeping them there is great reward. (Psalm 19:7-11)

The psalmist provides six synonyms for the Word of God, then gives six characteristics of that Word followed by six results of the Word in the lives of those who meditate upon that Word and pattern their lives by that Word. He concludes by promising that in the keeping of the Word of God is great reward (Psalm 19:7-11).

Six Ways We Will Be Restored When We Meditate

We spoke in an earlier chapter about Rhonda's radical restoration after she was delivered from drugs and alcohol through the power of God's Word. The Word will restore us in the same radical way, when we become meditators. Let's examine more closely the changes that took place in her when the Spirit planted God's Word in her inner person. Note that a synonym is used in place of "Word" in each verse.

1. Revival and Restoration

The law of the Lord is perfect, reviving the soul. (Psalm 19:7)

The healing process transferred Rhonda from the law of sin and death to the law of life in the Spirit of Christ Jesus. God revealed His perfect law — His deliverance, His bringing us into all His promises, and His commands, which are for our good — to her inner person.

God gave Moses the law as the perfect way to live. God's laws are the laws of love, intended for our highest good and the good of others. His perfect law of love brings us into perfect relationships, perfect balance and joy in our lives.

Then our lives become as sure and certain as the rising of the sun in the early morning.

The Apostle James puts it this way, "But one who looks into the perfect law, the law of liberty, and perseveres, being no hearer who forgets but a doer who acts, he will be blessed in his doing." (James 1:25) *Looking into* the perfect law of liberty, gazing intently at that law, is to *meditate* on that law. James compares it to looking at oneself in a mirror, gazing upon, pondering, reflecting, filling one's mind and heart with God's perfect law.

Revival is the result! God breathed His new life into Rhonda's spirit and restored her soul. The Word of God, which had taken up residence within her inner person, not only healed her infirmity but also restored her in mind, body and spirit.

We also will be restored. We will be made whole as we begin to meditate. All of our past wounds and scars from a lifestyle of neglect of God's Word and rebellion against His purposes in our lives will be removed and replaced with God's *shalom*—His wholeness and peace.

2. Walking In Wisdom

The testimony of the Lord is sure, making wise the simple. (Psalm 19:7)

The Bible is the testimony about God in Christ, the witness to Jesus Christ. Jesus Himself is the true Word of God, the *Faithful Witness* to God, (Revelation 1:5) and all the words of Scripture—the entire Bible both Old and New Testaments—witness to Jesus Christ as the only Savior and Lord of all nations. "For the testimony of Jesus is the spirit of prophecy," declares the Apostle John in Revelation 19:10. All prophecy, indeed the entire Bible, is a witness to God's saving grace in Christ Jesus, our Lord.

The witness of the Word of God has been proven over and over throughout two millennia and continues to be reliable and believable in this third millennium. This testimony to Jesus is dependable. We can base our lives upon this true witness and walk with confidence and certainty, just as a majestic mountain goat walks with sure-footed steps on a rocky hillside.

The testimony of the Lord leads to wisdom. "Let the word of Christ dwell in you richly," Paul writes, "teaching and admonishing one another in all wisdom, singing psalms and hymns and spiritual songs, with thankfulness in your hearts to God." (Colossians 3:16)

Wisdom was the gift that enabled Rhonda to discipline her life after her healing, to return to school and continue to grow in her new life in Christ. Her life began to be marked by the "wisdom from above . . . [which is] first pure, then peaceable, gentle, open to reason, full of mercy and good fruits, impartial and sincere." (James 3:17) She continued to become aware of God's wisdom, the wisdom of the cross, coming to a fuller understanding of the richness of her salvation because of Christ's sacrifice, thereby gaining the ability to apply her new knowledge of Jesus Christ to the situations that confronted her.

God's wisdom will come to us as we make our home in God's Word. Meditation is the secret of allowing the Word of Christ to richly dwell within us.[2] Some time ago I became aware of a new depth of wisdom in the life of my wife, Ellen. Her speech was becoming wiser, her relating to people deeper and her counseling ministry more effective. I did not have to search long to discover the reason for this growing wisdom. Long a meditator, she had just completed meditating through Paul's letter to the *Philippians,* verse-by-verse, line-by-line, a verse a day for over three months. The sure Word of God *made wise the simple,* just as the psalmist promised. The term "simple," when used in the Psalms, refers to an open-minded person, one willing to learn.

We have said in an earlier chapter that meditaton and study are different but that they complement each other. Bible study without meditation can become dry and arid, like a wind-blown desert. But meditation without reverent study of the Bible is even more dangerous, causing the meditator to go astray, falling into deep pits of emotionalism and even mysticism. Meditation is not fruitful without careful, diligent study of the Bible. Each needs the other. Meditation is the fruit of a life committed to knowing God through His Word.[3]

When we study and meditate on the words of Scripture, we are seeking to learn with both our minds and our hearts. We allow the Spirit of God to teach us, not to get a quick word to teach or exhort other people, but rather to enrich our own souls. Wisdom will be the result.

3. Filled With Joy

The precepts [statutes] of the Lord are right, rejoicing the heart. (Psalm 19:8)

A statute, or precept, is a prescribed boundary.

Shimei was a relative of King Saul who cursed and threw rocks at King David as he was fleeing the palace at the time of Absalom's insurrection. (2 Samuel 16:5-8) Rather than taking retribution against Shimei at that time, King David waited until he was dying and asked Solomon to deal wisely with the problem. Solomon later called Shimei and told him to build for himself a house in Jerusalem and live there, but never to go out beyond the boundaries of Jerusalem. He prescribed a boundary with the threat of death if Shemei were to cross over. Everything went well with Shimei for three years, even though he must have grown restless at being restricted to the city limits of Jerusalem. Perhaps he forgot all about the statute when he finally left the gates of Jerusalem to search for runaway servants, crossing the prescribed boundary set by Solomon. But the King did not forget. Shimei's reward was death.

The Word of God is a prescribed boundary for Christian living. In it is a proper boundary for everything—the use of money, the enjoyment of sex and the use of power. A life lived within these prescribed boundaries brings growth in right relationships, and growth brings great joy.

Rhonda, healed by the Word of God, restored by the perfect law of God and beginning to grow in wisdom, learned through the Word to live within the boundaries God had prescribed for her. Her former life was lived almost entirely outside the boundaries of God's Word, and she had paid the price. Now she began to live in a new way, understanding that previously what seemed to be boundaries that limited her freedom were in fact good and right foundations that gave her freedom to grow. And she was filled with joy.

4. Understanding God's Will for Our Lives

The commandment of the Lord is pure, enlightening the eyes. (Psalm 19:8).

God gives commands, not suggestions, but all His commands are for our highest welfare. He alone knows what is perfectly good for us, and obedience to His commandments will lead us into the knowledge of His will for our lives—His good, well pleasing and perfect will. (Romans 12:2)

Every command of God in the Scriptures is to be obeyed immediately, without delay, completely, and joyfully, as Joy Dawson always told those of us who were her students in YWAM (Youth With A Mission). God wants His people to meditate not only on the promises of His Word but also on His commands. "O how I love your law! It is my medita-

tion all the day. Your commandment makes me wiser than
my enemies, for it is ever with me," sang the psalmist.
(Psalm 119:97-98) The most fruitful meditation focuses on
the commands of God, not just His promises, because His
commands bring us into the very center of His wonderful
will for our lives.

The commandments of the Lord are *pure*. King David
says in another psalm that "the words of the Lord are pure
words, like silver refined in a furnace on the ground, purified
seven times." (Psalm 12:6) His words are clear and pure.
They have been tested and proven to be effective.

As God's Word began to break through Rhonda's hard
outer shell and take up residence within her, she gradually
became aware of the commandments of the Lord, and as she
began to obey those commands her eyes were opened, her
heart enlightened. Her understanding of God's perfect will
for her life began to unfold, just as a flower unfolds gradually in the light from the sun's rays. Each time we meditate, it is as if rays of sunlight flood down upon the page of
Scripture and then flow into our hearts and bathe us in the
healing, enlightening light of God.

5. Living Life With an Eternal Quality

The fear of the Lord is clean, enduring forever (Psalm
19:9).

The psalmist calls God's Word "the fear of the Lord."
Throughout the Scriptures we are exhorted to walk in the
fear of the Lord. What does it mean, then, to have the "fear
of the Lord" in our lives? To stand in the fear of the Lord
means three things:

- First, it is to stand before God's objective Word of
  truth, embracing God's Word as the sole standard
  and authority for life, and seeking to let that Word
  dwell in us richly.

- Second, it means to submit every area of our lives to that Word, allowing it to break us and purify us by leading us away from sin and evil and towards God, remolding us into the image of Jesus Christ.
- Finally, it means to stand in awe at His majesty, filled with wonder and expectation of His mighty deeds, both humbled and thrilled at the awareness that He desires to perform His mighty works through us.[4]

Early Church Christians lived their lives in the fear of the Lord. At Pentecost the Holy Spirit descended upon the believers in power like a mighty wind, and in tongues of fire to cleanse and burn away sin from their lives. They lived their lives in the power of the Spirit, constantly aware that He was the Spirit of holiness. Luke reports that "awe came upon every soul, and many wonders and signs were being done through the apostles." (Acts 2:43) The fear of the Lord is clean, separate from all evil, and will lead God's people into a life of freedom that stands ready to do His will.

The fear of the Lord endures forever, and the Scriptures promise that one who lives in the fear of the Lord will live a longer, more balanced and fruitful life. Surely God intervened at the perfect time into Rhonda's life, delivering her from the snare of drugs and alcohol, the snare set for her by the Enemy of her soul. What could have been a short, tragic life was transformed instead into a life that is now being lived in the light of eternity, marked by an eternal quality that blesses other people.

6. Living a Righteous Life and Understanding God's Justice

The rules (judgments) of the Lord are true, and righteous altogether (Psalm 19:9).

The Word of God is certain; it is true. No other book in the entire world contains the whole truth about God. Only

God's Word, the Bible, is truth. As Jesus is the truth incarnate so the Bible, the only infallible witness to Jesus, is His truth incarnate in words. The Bible reveals the rules of God for all human relationships, both for individuals and for nations. Those rules reveal the justice of God for all people, for the poor and oppressed, the needy and outcast. It contains God's judgment on human beings' cruelty and inhumanity towards one another.

The result of allowing God's Word to reshape our thinking, to re-form our approach to life, will be a just society where the orphan and the widow are cared for, where the homeless and deprived, the afflicted and the alienated are restored to a higher quality of living in the light of God's justice.

Bible meditation is the key to enduring social change. Daily coming into the presence of God's Word and allowing Him to speak personally into our lives through His Word— His plan and agenda for our personal lives and for the world—will bring life to a world that is following the path of self-destruction. Meditation does not lead us into withdrawal from involvement in the world; rather, through meditation we enter into communion with the Lord who walks among all the nations and peoples of the world to bring the Father's justice to all humankind.

God's Word Brings Total Restoration and Reformation.

What God did through His Word for Rhonda, as she lay captive to Satan's stronghold of drugs and alcohol, He is ready to do for everyone. He will bring renewal and restoration into our lives as well, as we allow His Word to make its home in us through regular meditation. His Word will:

Renew our thoughts: We will begin to think like God thinks, freed from a negative, destructive thought pattern to a positive, life-giving way of thinking.

Redirect our wills: Meditation will lead us away from self-centered living into a life of total submission to God, seeking His will above all else.

Restore our emotions: No one is totally free from inner wounds or twisted emotions; yet the Word of God promises healing and restoration of emotions.

Refocus our imaginations: Fantasies that produce unrealistic expectations and often destructive behavior will be replaced by true vision from God, as we begin to use our imagination for God's glory alone.

Replenish our nourishment: Fed by God Himself each day, our lives will become healthy and well balanced, bearing fruit in every circumstance.

Rebuke our sin: Daily meditation on the Word of God will give strength to break bondages to sin and redirect us into obedience and freedom in Christ.

Rejoice our spirits: Depression, despair, loss of desire and apathy will be replaced by freedom and an inner joy that rises above outward circumstances.

Re-energize our bodies: Dwelling daily in the presence of the Lord will bring new life and vitality to our bodies as well as our souls. Tired muscles and weak limbs can be restored, even diseases healed, through constant abiding in the presence of the Divine Physician, by meditating on His Word. Medical science itself attests to the value of the combined disciplines of spiritual meditation and physical exercise.

Redeem our lives: The Word of God will deliver us from all oppression and enslavement to Satan and his angels and will establish us firmly in His righteousness, enabling us to grow into the mature men and women that He desires us to be.

No wonder, then, that the psalmist concluded his praise of the Word of God by saying that God's words are "more to be desired than gold, even much fine gold; sweeter also than honey and drippings of the honeycomb . . .. In keeping them there is great reward!" (Psalm 19:10-11)

Invitation to the Banquet Table
Personal Meditation on Psalm 139

1. Review the four simple steps of meditation.
First, prepare your heart.
Second, listen to all God wants to say to you through
the text.
Third, seek to meet God as He reveals Himself to you.
Fourth, respond to Him in prayer and obedience

2. Read through the entire chapter of Psalm 139.
Open yourself to God and listen as you read.
Try to understand what the psalmist wants to express
through this psalm.

3. Meditate on Psalm 139, **verse 13.**
For you formed my inward parts;
You knitted me together in my mother's womb.
Allow God to lead you into the deep mystery of your life
through this verse.
Use your imagination to see Him knitting you together in
your mother's womb.
Listen to what the Lord wants to say to you personally!

4. Write down in your Meditation Journal what the Lord
says to you.
Or you may write out your prayer to Him.
Allow the Spirit to lead you as you listen to the Lord.

5. Take time now to *wait upon the Lord*.
Give Him your heart. Ask Him to reveal Himself to you.

6. Spend time in prayer.
Thank God for His word to you.
Commit yourself to obeying Him.

Chapter Eleven

The Sin-Destroying Word

> "I have stored up your word in my heart,
> that I might not sin against you."
> Psalm 119:11

God's plan for us is wholeness, not incompleteness or fragmented living. His life in us abounds in peace and hope, not destruction. (Jeremiah 29:11) But Satan opposes God's plan and seeks to destroy us. His greatest tool is not persecution, neither is it sickness nor economic deprivation. No, Satan's most effective tool against the well-meaning Christian is the Christian's own thought life!

We have spoken of Rhonda, the young girl who was delivered and healed from mental illness by listening to the Word of God one hour a day for six months.[1] It was her own thought life, deceived by Satan, that nearly caused her death. Her sins and wounded spirit became the platform for the enemy's attacks. What was true of Rhonda is true of all. Our sins are rooted in evil, sinful thoughts that, if not checked, inevitably will lead to destruction. Our wounded spirits are based on unworthy thoughts that harbor resentment and lead to low self-esteem that inhibits fruitful, productive lives in society.

The renewal of the Christian's thought life is a theme that runs continuously through Paul's writings. We are told to put away the clothes of the old life and dress in the new clothes of the Gospel, being renewed in heart, mind and will. But it is Luke who reveals to us most pointedly the danger of an unrenewed mind.

Luke begins the twenty-second chapter of his Gospel with an account of the Jewish religious leaders' plot to kill Jesus. In this critical moment Jesus shares His last meal with His disciples, perhaps the most intimate of their times together. Yet deep irony runs throughout this story. The disciples, during their final fellowship meal with their Lord, actually argued as to who would be regarded as the greatest among them! The irony goes nearly beyond imagination, disputing as to which of them would become the greatest leader while sitting in the presence of the one true Servant Leader!

Only the servant of all can be the leader of all, Jesus teaches them. Their way is not the secular, worldly way of authority based on power or age or position. No, He reminds them, "I am among you as the one who serves." (Luke 22:24-34)

Jesus does indeed promise them a place in His coming Kingdom. He actually promises to give them His whole Kingdom! Yet they would be satisfied rather with mere worldly position by competing among themselves for authority. Clearly they are not yet able to appropriate the full blessing of spiritual authority that He intends to give them.

"Simon, Simon, behold, Satan demanded to have you, that he might sift you like wheat!" (Luke 23:31) Jesus is telling Simon Peter that He has given Satan permission to attack Peter, even to "sift him like wheat!" Satan's demand was actually a request, for Satan has no authority over Jesus to make a demand. But Jesus permitted Satan's attack because it was the *only way for Simon Peter to become prepared* for the great position of leadership, which Jesus would give him.

Dear reader, take comfort in the fact that the devil can never attack you without permission from the Lord of your life, the Lover of your soul. Once He gives permission, we have confidence that it is for our greater good, that we may be made more fruitful. God always has a purpose in allowing the Enemy to attack His people, and it is to make us stronger in Him.

Satan's Attacks

Satanic attacks are common as Christians plan and lay foundations for new ministries. The Book of Acts records the varied attacks of Satan directed towards the newly emerging Church. First came persecution, including physical attack. But the enemy's attacks only made the new Christians bolder and more determined to evangelize the world. The Church was purified and empowered! Christians today continue to experience similar persecution, but the Church of Jesus Christ remains strong!

Then came moral attacks, centered in Ananias and Sapphira. Their sins were the sins of *tokenism* and *deception,* desiring to be recognized as having committed themselves wholly while actually living selfishly. Throughout history, believers have been attacked in moral areas, especially areas such as money, sex and use of power. But God's plan is to use Satan's attacks to lead His people into deeper holiness and fruitful ministry. The Early Church entered a new level of holiness when they dealt with this sin.[2]

Having failed to destroy God's people through *persecution* and *moral attacks,* Satan turned to one of his most effective weapons: *distracting* the believer from his primary mission. A complaint arose on the part of the Greek-speaking Jews against the Hebrews because their widows were being neglected in the daily distribution of food.[3] Satan's purpose was to distract the Apostles from their primary mission of prayer and the ministry of the Word by causing them to be absorbed in the practical business details of the new Church. The New Testament Church, however, overcame this attack by appointing deacons, so that not only the Apostles but also all the believers could be *single-minded* in service to the Lord! This attack continues, and today's Church has yet to rediscover the great power of single-minded devotion to the Lord. Paul's appeal to the Corinthian Christians echoes again to the modern believer: " . . . but I am afraid that as the serpent deceived Eve by his cunning, *your thoughts will be led astray* from a sincere and pure devotion to Christ." (2 Corinthians 11:3)

The Christian's Husk-Nature

Jesus warned Simon Peter that Satan had been permitted to "sift him like wheat." Nevertheless we must remember that the purpose of sifting wheat is to remove the useless husks from the good kernel so that the wheat can be used for food. It may be that Satan is used by God to sift us like wheat, but what will emerge will be a life freed from the outer "husk-nature" and empowered to serve God in freedom and power.

What then is the Christian's "husk-nature?" It is the areas we hide in darkness—areas of uncrucified thoughts, wrong attitudes, unresolved sin. For Simon Peter, perhaps it was his pride and lust for power. Peter himself undoubtedly was unaware of this area of darkness within himself, hidden deeply beneath his consciousness. King David had a "husk-nature"—sexual lust—which lay dormant during the early part of his life, never dealt with until it surfaced and caused destruction in his kingdom. Jesus' disciples' "husk-nature" could have been their fear—fear of persecution or of commitment. The "husk-nature" is that vulnerable area in which Satan can attack.

Jesus asked Simon Peter, "Do you know the area of your life where you are vulnerable and where Satan can easily attack you?" And He asks us today. Do you know the area in your life where Satan can cause you to fall? Peter did not know, and for this reason God allowed Satan to attack him so that this husk-nature could be revealed and removed.

Jesus knew that Simon Peter would fail, but He had perfect confidence that Peter would recover and become stronger, so that he could strengthen his brothers. But first he had to undergo this severe testing of his faith. And Peter failed. He did not accept the warning from Jesus and denied that he was weak and vulnerable to Satan's attack. Peter did not know himself, which in itself was evidence of his deeply hidden pride.

In times of crisis or undue stress, these hidden areas inevitably will surface. Peter could not handle the disappointment of Jesus' arrest, so his "husk-nature" surfaced and he denied that he even knew Jesus. David was overwhelmed by his own success and prestige, as well as by the pressures of being king, and his "husk-nature" of sexual lust surfaced and resulted in adultery and murder.

Is this not a warning to all of God's servants? There is no one among us who does not have some hidden area of darkness which, were it to surface, would bring sorrow to our Lord and harm to His Kingdom. We must not be ignorant of these hidden areas of darkness in our lives. Jesus revealed this truth to Peter so that He could heal him. And He seeks to reveal our latent areas of sin so that we can acknowledge and repent of these areas and be used more greatly by Him.

Dealing With the Husk-Nature

The good news is that Jesus Himself is praying for us. Faced with denial from His beloved disciple, Jesus nevertheless told him that He had prayed for him that his faith might not fail! He further told Peter that He was confident that he would be restored, and that he would be enabled then to strengthen his brothers, who undoubtedly would go through the same trials. (Luke 22:32) The Apostle John confirms Jesus' promise: "My little children . . . if anyone does sin, we have an advocate with the Father, Jesus Christ the righteous." (1 John 2:1)

Good news indeed! Yet we must cooperate with Jesus and His Spirit to put to death completely these strongholds of Satan in our lives. How then do we deal with these areas of darkness in our thought life? There are four things we must do.

Knowing Who Planted the Thoughts.

First, we must know that it is Satan who has planted these dark thoughts in our minds. These negative thoughts are Satan's "counterfeit words" with which he attempts to replace God's words! We have cooperated with him, but he is the one who plants these thoughts in order to destroy us. How very different from the Spirit of God, who plants the thoughts of God in us, through His Word, in order to give us abundant life! We must know that we are engaged in a great warfare, and the great battlefield is our minds!

Being Honest With Ourselves.

Second, we must be brutally honest with ourselves. We must have a heart of love and passion for the Lord and a heart of compassion for others. But our heart towards ourselves must be one of steel.

We must acknowledge these areas of our husk-nature and never defend ourselves to cover our weaknesses. No more honest prayer can be found than that of David when he admitted his sin and asked God for a clean heart.[4] We must cooperate with the Holy Spirit as He seeks to reveal to us our inner thoughts, things about ourselves which we do not know.

Submitting Each Thought to Christ.

Third, we must submit each thought to the Lord Jesus Christ. Submission is the key to victory over Satan. "Submit yourselves therefore to God. Resist the devil, and he will flee from you," says James the Apostle. (James 4:7) Paul reminds us that the weapons that we use to do spiritual warfare are not fleshly but rather are mighty tools given to us by God to destroy the Enemy's strongholds. We take *every thought captive to obey Christ,* says Paul. Then he reminds us that we must first take our own thoughts captive and submit each one to Christ, before we can resist Satan and his great attacks on the thought life of the world, especially of our generation. (2 Corinthians 10:3-6)

What are the thoughts that each believer must take captive and submit to Jesus Christ? These are the thoughts that comprise the negative thought patterns that we have developed over many years. We have "meditated" on these negative thoughts for many years, and we have become what we have been thinking! We can divide these thoughts into two groups: *sinful* thoughts and *unworthy* thoughts.

Sinful Thoughts. Consider these sinful thoughts and see if you can discover any in your own life:

- *Lustful thoughts*—seeking self-gratification through ways that do not please God;
- *Judgmental thoughts*—classifying people and condemning them, refusing to enter into their pain or suffering;
- *Jealous, envious thoughts*—resenting others who receive something or are able to do something I feel I should receive or be able to do;
- *Competitive thoughts*—comparing ourselves with others and trying to prove to God and others that I am better;
- *Manipulative thoughts*—attempting to use other people to my advantage in order to secure a position or receive some reward;
- *Critical and proud thoughts*—unwilling to see others' viewpoints; making myself the center of all things;
- *Hateful thoughts*— nurturing my anger and holding it in rather than dealing with it.

Do you recognize any thoughts in yourself that need to be taken captive and submitted to Christ?

Unworthy Thoughts. Consider now the unworthy thoughts which lead us into self-deception and self-hatred:

- *I am a failure*—nothing works out for me; I am not able to perform.
- *I am just a sinner*—the greatest excuse for sinning.
- *I am afraid*—afraid of myself, afraid to trust God.
- *I am not worthy*—seeing no value in myself, rather having to find value in what I do.
- *I hate myself*—self-rejection.
- *I am alone. Nobody cares*—self-pity, blinding us from God's love and from others' desire to be part of our lives.
- *I don't care anymore*—bitterness, anger at disappointing circumstances or rejection.

- *I'm just going to give up—* losing the desire to do anything or to have expectations of others.
- *I don't want to talk about it*—refusing to be open; closing myself off from others.

These are negative thoughts which have been planted by Satan, but which we have nourished. And no one is without some of these sinful or unworthy thoughts, even though we may not be consciously in touch with them. We must repent of each thought, and be forgiven and cleansed by the blood of Jesus Christ. Then God will remove these thoughts.

But what happens after the Christian repents and is cleansed? You may recall Jesus' story of the unclean spirit who goes out of a person, then seeks a place to rest but finds none. The spirit returns to the house from which it came and finds that it has been swept clean, empty and put in order. Then it goes and brings with it seven other spirits more evil than itself. (Matthew 12:43-45) So it is with one who repents of evil thoughts, planted by Satan, and who is cleansed and emptied of these thoughts. Nature abhors a vacuum, and so does the spiritual world. In order to be freed completely from these evil thoughts, which would destroy us, we must take the fourth step in dealing with the husk-nature.

Planting New Thoughts Through Bible Meditation.

Fourth, then, is to plant new thoughts through Bible meditation. These thoughts will replace the old thoughts from Satan that have caused us to be negative in our thinking and in our whole worldview. But how do we plant new thoughts? Remember that it is the *Spirit of God* who plants the seed of the Word in us each time we meditate. As we meditate each morning or evening, we must welcome the Spirit who desires to accomplish this great work in us. As we focus on the words of the Biblical text, we open ourselves to God's

Spirit, and allow Him to plant those words in us. Then the Word becomes alive and active in us, to destroy the remnants of sin that contaminate us and prevent us from being used more greatly for the extension of God's Kingdom.

"I have stored up your word in my heart, that I might not sin against you," proclaims the psalmist. (Psalm 119:11) Again he speaks of the righteous person: "The law of his God is in his heart; his steps do not slip. " (Psalm 37:31) The writers of the Psalms knew well the power of the Word of God in overcoming the attacks of Satan.

As we seek to be rid of the sins and hurts within us by meditating on the Word of God, we must do so in the context of on-going reading of the Scriptures as well as memorization of passages of the Bible. As we read we become aware of the whole truth of God, and this truth begins to free us from our bondages and sets us free. As we memorize passages of Scripture, our minds are filled with the words of truth. Then, as we meditate, the truth that is in our understanding, in our minds, becomes experiential truth that rests in our hearts as well. When we meditate we always do so with the prayer that we might be remolded by the Word of God, just as clay is molded by the potter, so that we become more like Christ, hating sin and loving righteousness.

The Spirit of God knows our hearts. He knows all that is in our minds. For this reason, we do not need to choose selective passages that we think would fill the void of thoughts that have been taken captive and submitted to Christ. For example, a believer who is constantly bothered by thoughts of unworthiness or weakness does not need to choose verses that speak of the power we have in Christ. Of course these verses will help. But because the Spirit knows what we need even more than we do, we simply submit ourselves to Him. Rather than randomly choosing verses of Scripture that we think fit our needs, we would be wise to meditate with regularity on a book of the Bible or on a chapter of the Bible that we have chosen, always remembering that meditation has the most power when we ponder over each word, a verse a day. The meditator on the Scriptures, who follows the sequence of the chapter or book on which he is meditating verse by verse, is constantly awed by the appropriateness of each day's meditation to his daily life and needs. The reason for this is that the Spirit of God applies our daily meditation to the deepest needs and yearnings of our hearts!

An example of this would be Philippians, chapter four. Paul comforts us with this word: "I can do all things through Him who strengthens me." (Philippians 4:13) This is a powerful word for the believer who is entrapped in his own weakness. Yet rather than meditating just on this one verse in isolation, how much better it is to meditate on the entire chapter! If we do this, then we will not take specific verses out of context. More importantly, the entire chapter four of Philippians will encourage the weak Christian to be strong in the Lord. Better yet, meditate on the *entire book* of Philippians, a verse or a sentence a day. And you will discover that, as the Spirit plants this dynamic word in you, you will begin to move in His power that overcomes sin and weakness.

Bible meditation is one of the great tools for spiritual warfare! Yet how often we neglect this basic tool and attempt to confront the enemy out of our own understanding or imagination, or simply with new and creative methods that often have beautiful form while lacking content and power. Then we wonder why we have no power over the Enemy.

We must bear the image of Christ within us before we can effectively confront the Enemy with our words. And it is meditation that opens the door for the Spirit to remold us into the image of Christ. The great truth of spiritual warfare is that the Christian himself, remolded into the image of Christ, is God's greatest tool for defeating the Enemy. Jesus Christ is the Victor! The Spirit of Christ in us defeated the

Enemy on Calvary and is greater than all the powers of earth or hell! (1John 4:4)

Dear believer, continue to meditate on the Word of God on a daily basis. Then, in place of depression, you will find the joy of the Lord. Instead of unbelief, Christ will reveal Himself alive in you and faith will well up within your heart as you draw from the wells of salvation. (Isaiah 12:4) Love of sin will be replaced by love for the Lord. And all fears will be removed by the transforming love of God!

Invitation to the Banqueting Table
Personal Meditation on Psalm 139

1. Review the four simple steps of meditation.
First, prepare your heart.
Second, listen to all God wants to say to you through the text.
Third, seek to meet God as He reveals Himself to you.
Fourth, respond to Him in prayer and obedience

2. Read through the entire chapter of Psalm 139.
Open yourself to God and listen as you read.
Try to understand what the psalmist wants to express through this psalm.

3. Meditate on Psalm 139, **verse 14.**
I praise you, for I am fearfully and wonderfully made.
Wonderful are your works; my soul knows it very well.
Listen to God as He describes how He created you.
Concentrate on your inner being, not just your physical form.
Invite the Holy Spirit to speak into your spirit—Spirit to spirit.
Ask God to reveal to you how He sees you.

Praise God for His wonderful work in creating you.

4. Write down in your Meditation Journal what the Lord
says to you.
Or you may write out your prayer to Him.
Allow the spirit to lead you as you listen to the Lord.

5. Take time now to *wait upon the Lord*.
Give Him your heart. Ask Him to reveal Himself to you.

6. Spend time in prayer.
Thank God for His word to you. Commit yourself to obey
Him.

Chapter Twelve

The Conquering Word

"... You are strong, and the Word of God abides in you,
and you have overcome the evil one."
I John 2:14b

W hen the Spirit of God implants His words in us through
our regular and sustained meditation, we are empowered by those words to become all that God wants us to be
and to do all that God desires us to do. They are the words of
God's power, resting deep within our inner beings.

The Christian's strength, claims the Apostle John, lies in
the Word of God thus implanted. "I write to you, young men
[and women]," says John, "because you are strong, and the
Word of God abides in you, and you have overcome the evil
one." (1 John 2:14) The growing Christian is strong because
he abides in the Word of God, the same Word that Jesus
speaks to uphold the entire universe, the Word that flows out
of God's power.

The apostle Paul thanked God that the Christians of
Thessalonica received the Word of God not as the word of
men "but for what it really is, the Word of God, which also

performs its work in you who believe." (1 Thessalonians 2:13) Behind the Word of God on which we meditate daily lies the power of God to transform lives, to free from oppression, liberate from bondages and reshape our lives until the image of Jesus Christ is formed within each believer.

The Holy Spirit works through that Word to build us up and bring us into the full inheritance of the children of God. That word is so powerful that Paul, giving his farewell address to the elders of the Church at Ephesus, concluded by saying, " . . . and now I commend you to God and to the word of His grace, which is able to build you up and to give you the inheritance among all those who are sanctified." (Acts 20:32) As we have said in an earlier chapter, he did not commit the Word to them but rather them to the Word, the Word of God's power and grace. It is upon that Word that we are commanded to meditate "day and night," so that we can be prepared to be God's instruments, His "overcomers," in the world. Now let's meet a man who did that very thing, a man who staked his life on the Word of God and became a conqueror of nations through that Word.

Joshua the Seeker

As a young man Joshua was a warrior, but he was more than that. He earned the trust of Moses to such a degree that Moses shared with him his most intimate times with the Lord. Moses alone, of all the people of Israel, was invited by the Lord to come "near to the Lord," into His actual presence. When he went up the mountain to meet the Lord for forty days and nights and receive the blueprint of the tabernacle—its pattern including all the furnishings and even the garments of the priests—all the elders of the people, including Aaron the high priest, were instructed to wait at the foot of the mountain.

But he took his young assistant Joshua with him, saying to the elders, "wait here for us until we return to you." (Exodus 24:13-14) Only Joshua, of all the people of Israel, was able to share this time of intimacy with Moses and with the Lord. Later, Moses would go regularly into the "tent of meeting" to meet the Lord. There the Lord would speak to Moses "face to face, as a man speaks to his friend!" Joshua, a young man who already had experienced the presence of the Lord, was invited to follow Moses into the tent and remain with him as Moses and the Lord talked intimately.

Is it any wonder, then, that when Moses would leave the tent and return to the camp, the young man, Joshua, would not leave? (Joshua 33:7-11) He remained behind. He waited upon the Lord who had spoken to Moses. He longed to hear that same voice of the Lord calling his name, speaking to him, sharing with him the intimacies that God reserves for those who seek Him, who fear His name, who long for Him as the deer longs for running water.

The heart of the young man, Joshua, is the heart of every true child of God who longs to meet God face to face, to hear Him speak of "great and hidden things which [he] has not known." (Jeremiah 33:3) Had Joshua lived during the time of Jesus' life on earth, he would have rejoiced greatly at the invitation Jesus gave to His disciples and which He gives today to all who follow Him: "No longer do I call you servants, for the servant does not know what his master is doing; but I have called you friends, for all that I have heard from My Father I have made known to you!" (John 15:15)

God was preparing Joshua for greatness. There would be a time in the future when God would use Joshua to complete the salvation of delivering His people from bondage in Egypt to enjoy all the promises of God in the Promised Land. He was being prepared to lead God's people into their full inheritance, not just individually but corporately as a nation. Moses was aware of God's training program for young Joshua and encouraged him to seek the Lord steadfastly, to listen to Him when He spoke, to make intimacy with the Lord his goal in life. And Joshua did just that. He was ready when God elevated him to the next stage of his journey.

Joshua the Meditator

"Moses My servant is dead." Moses, who had commanded and pleaded with the people of Israel to "walk after the Lord your God and fear Him and keep His commandments and obey His voice . . . serve Him and hold fast to Him," (Deuteronomy 13:4) was no longer the leader of the people. "Now therefore arise," the Lord said to Joshua, "go over this Jordan, you and all this people, into the land that I am giving to them, to the people of Israel!" (Joshua 1:1-2)

The first chapter of the Book of Joshua gives in detail the many promises that God gave to Joshua: the promise that he would possess great areas of land by conquering nations greater and mightier than Israel, in fulfillment of the promises God previously had made to Abraham and to Moses; the promise of strength and leadership; the promise that He would never fail or desert Joshua, that He would cause him to be successful in the task given him; and the greatest promise of all Scripture, that God Himself would be with him and never leave him.

But all these promises depended on the commands that God gave to Joshua. Throughout chapter one, God commands Joshua to "be strong and courageous . . . do not be frightened and do not be dismayed . . . be careful to obey fully the law which Moses commanded you." All these commands are summed up in these words: "This Book of the Law shall not depart from your mouth, but you shall meditate on it day and night, so that you may be careful to do according to all that is written in it. For then you will make your way prosperous, and then you will have good success." (Joshua 1:8)

Here it is, the command which will open the way for Joshua to lead the people of Israel, that great unruly mob of between two and three million insubordinate, rebellious, complaining people, into the promised land: "You shall *meditate* on this book of the law day and night!"[1]

No other command is given. Joshua was simply to meditate day and night on the Book of the Law. This command may strike most modern readers as overly simplistic and even as unrealistic. Faced with such a formidable task today, surely one would immediately begin by seeking substantial financial backing, procuring at least a master's degree in business administration from a leading university and calling a consultation to outline the goals and explore strategies for achieving them. But while these steps may or may not be necessary in some situations, God gave Joshua only one command: *Meditate.*

Joshua was not taken by surprise when God told him that the way to become a conqueror of nations was first to become a meditator. Joshua already was a meditator. He had meditated on God's law from youth, he had sought the nearness of God, tarried in His presence, longed to hear His voice in the night watches and the stillness before the break of day. He knew the secret known by all the men and women whom God has used mightily, whether in the Scriptures or in more modern history. God works through meditators. All ministry that is blessed and anointed by God begins with meditaton. Joshua was prepared to allow the Spirit of God to further empower him for his task, through daily meditation on His Word.

"This Book of the Law ..."

Joshua was told to meditate daily on the book of the law. He was not instructed by God to focus only on all the promises, to meditate day and night on all that God had said He would do for him. He was commanded rather to meditate on the law.

To the Christian, to the one who has been born again into a living hope, into eternal life, not by the law but by the grace of God in His sacrifice of His Son, Jesus Christ, this is good news. This is what we are supposed to be doing day and night, filling our minds and hearts with God's perfect law, longing to please Him and live obediently at the center of His will. Paul said it most succinctly: "And He died for all, that they who live might no longer live for themselves but for Him who for their sakes died and was raised." (2 Corinthians 5:15)

Having been freed from the demands of the law for salvation, the true Christian is now able to love the law, to rejoice in the law, to seek to obey the law of God in the power of the Holy Spirit, all for the glory of the Father. The Scriptures give no more powerful object of meditation than the law of God. In keeping the law there is great reward; all the promises of God are poured out upon those who delight in God's perfect will. The psalmist expresses the heart of the believer when he exclaims, "Oh how I love Your law! It is my meditation all the day." (Psalm 119:97)

The Perfect Law of Liberty

But just what is the "perfect law of liberty," as the apostle James describes it? Moses, who first received the law directly from God, raised the question himself in the Book of Deuteronomy. Your son will ask you in time to come, he said, saying, "What is the meaning of the testimonies and the statutes and the rules that the Lord our God has commanded you?"

This "Book of the Law" on which God told Joshua to meditate was not simply the moral teachings or the ethical standards of God, important as these are. No, it certainly included these but was much larger and more inclusive. Moses told the people of Israel to teach their sons and daughters the Law of God in the following way: *First,* "The Lord brought us out of Egypt with a mighty hand;" *second,* "He brought us out from there, that He might bring us in and give us the land that He swore to give to our fathers;" *third,* "And the Lord commanded us to do all these statutes, to fear the Lord our God, for our good always." (Deuteronomy 6:20-25)

Here, then, is the perfect law of God: God's deliverance, God's promises and God's commands. No one truly knows the law of God who does not know the deliverance and the salvation of God, and the promises that come to those who believe. The Bible tells us of the *completed work of salvation in Jesus Christ,* of His delivering us from sin, and it tells us of His forgiveness and reconciliation which we receive by faith. It reminds us that God cares for us as a loving heavenly Father, and that He has prepared a rich inheritance for us together with all believers of all ages. After we have been saved through grace by the sacrifice of Jesus Christ on Calvary, then, and only then, we are able to hear and rejoice in the commands of God.[2]

The Bible alone, of all the books in the world, tells the complete story of God's deliverance and salvation, His promises, His commands. So it is on the *whole Word of God* that we are to meditate. Whenever we read the phrase "this Book of the Law" in Moses' writings or in the Psalms, we can understand that we are surely to meditate on *the whole Word of God.* But remember that, although we certainly may, and must, meditate on all the promises and provisions of the Lord, our greatest joy is to meditate on His will for our lives and to walk in obedience to Him. For this reason one of the most fruitful passages for meditation in the entire Bible is Psalm 119. We will speak of this psalm again later, but consider setting aside at least ten or fifteen minutes a day for the next six months and meditating on Psalm 119, one verse a day, until you reach the end (verse 176). Your life will be transformed, your thinking renewed, your emotions refocused, your will redirected. And you will begin to sing with the psalmist, "Oh how I love your law! It is my meditation all the day." (Psalm 119:97)

Communion and Communication

Meditation on the Word of God was the key to Joshua's victory in leading Israel into the Promised Land. Two things prove that to be true. One is that regular meditation opens the door to *communion,* or intimacy, with the Lord. It is in our daily abiding in the Word that we enter deeply into that sweet fellowship of His presence and come to know Him intimately. As we commune with the Lord we come to know His heart, we are bathed in His love and restored in our souls, filled with joy and refreshed in spirit. We are ready to begin the day's tasks. Joshua knew well that his time of communion with the Lord was the source of all his authority and power to lead the people of God. Intimacy with the Lord is the secret of all ministry. *"From Me comes your fruit,"* says the Lord. (Hosea 14:6)

The other reason meditation was the key for Joshua's being able to become a conqueror is that meditation opens the door for *communication* with God. God desired to speak to Joshua each morning, before Joshua spoke to the leaders of his nation. Listening to the Lord is the heart of meditation. *"Lord, what is it You desire to say to me today?"* This is where we begin.

Each morning, God would awaken Joshua and, as Joshua listened, would speak to him of "great and hidden things" which He planned to do through Joshua and through the nation of Israel. He spoke to Joshua of His love for him. He spoke to him just like He had spoken to Moses, as a "man speaks to a friend." And He gave him his marching orders for that day, which Joshua then related to the leaders of the people.

Here is the reason meditation on the Word of God is the key to the victorious Christian life even today! This is why meditation is the key to all ministry. The reason is that the very same two things that happened to Joshua when he meditated—entering into deep communion with God and receiving direct communication from God—will happen to us as well, when we meditate. God desires to meet us in His Word, to share fellowship and communion with us. He longs to renew us with His presence. Then He desires to speak to us each day, to communicate His love and His plan for our lives.

What great joy this brings the believer, to realize that the same God who met Moses and spoke to Him in deep intimacy, as a Friend, desires to meet us in the same way, and speak to us as we listen. Moses, as he concluded his final sermon, exclaimed, "Indeed, He loves His people; all His holy ones are in His hand; they lie down at His feet and receive His words."[3]

Two Things Needed Each Day

Alone with God. Joshua needed to do two things each day in order to become a meditator. First, he had to set aside a certain time to be *alone with God.* This time alone with God was his single most important priority in any given day; indeed the remainder of the day depended on his setting this time aside to be with God. This was the time to meet God, to enter into His presence, to turn away from temptations, doubts and fears that naturally assailed him as a leader of his people. Joshua was aware that the greater the leadership responsibilities, the greater the attacks of Satan. This was the time to open himself fully before the Lord, to invite the Lord to enter into every area of his life—into his weaknesses, his loneliness—a time of healing and restoration, a time of deep and intimate fellowship with the Lord.

As we begin to meditate we will come to agree with Joshua that nothing must supplant this time alone with God each morning; we will come to guard jealously this time against all other interruptions, for this is our appointment with God! Remember, dear reader, you must come into God's presence alone, no one else but you. You need no other books to assist you in coming into the presence of the Lord, just the Bible. If listening to music helps you, it should be music that does not distract you. This is a precious time of meeting between your Lord and you, with no one else. Your ministry begins with this time. Indeed all ministry flows from the depth of fellowship with the Lord that is made possible by spending time alone with Him.

Silence. The other thing Joshua had to do each day was to learn to be silent as he came into the presence of the Lord. He had to bring his soul into a quiet stillness before the Lord and listen to all that He had to say to him.

Silence is not merely the absence of sound. It is not a passive emptiness waiting to be filled. Rather, silence is fullness, the place where God dwells. To be silent is to enter into the presence of God with an aggressive attitude of listening, longing to hear His voice, ready to do His will.

Joshua was aware that servanthood, or discipleship, begins with listening. He would have agreed with the apostle Paul who gave the following advice to young Timothy:

> *But as for you, continue in what you have learned and have firmly believed . . .. From childhood you have been acquainted with the sacred writings, which are able to make you wise for salvation through faith in Jesus Christ. All Scripture is breathed out by God*

*and profitable for teaching, for reproof, for
correction, and for training in righteousness, that the man of God may be competent,
equipped for every good work.*
(2 Timothy 3:14-17)

Nothing is more important for the believer than to learn
to listen to God as He speaks each day. The words that He
speaks will bring life and power, and great understanding;
they will enable us to enter fully into the inheritance He has
provided for all who rest secure in His love.

Joshua the Conqueror

So Joshua became the conqueror of all the lands and
peoples who were much mightier and more powerful than
the small and seemingly insignificant band of Israelites.
He became a conqueror because he first became a seeker,
a listener to God, a meditator on the words that God had
spoken previously to Moses and now was speaking to him.

The Book of Joshua records his life story from the time
of Moses' death to his own death. It tells of his great love for
and complete submission to God's Word; it reveals how his
life and the life of his people were completely transformed
and reformed through that Word. At one point he built an
altar to the Lord on Mount Ebal and on the altar carved into
the stones the whole Book of the Law. He then divided all
the people of Israel into two groups, half standing in front
of Mount Gerizim and half in front of Mount Ebal; there he
read all the words of the law, the blessing and the curse, just
as Moses had instructed him to do. Joshua so loved the law
that "there was not a word . . . that Joshua did not read before
all the assembly of Israel, and the women, and the little ones,
and the sojourners who lived among them!"[4]

You can read for yourself the account of his unprecedented conquests in the Book of Joshua. But as you read, focus your attention on what it was that enabled him to become such a conqueror. It was the Word of God. It was Joshua's longing to come daily into the presence of God and be renewed. It was Joshua's clinging to God and to His Word, constantly listening to every word that God would speak, and then submitting himself fully to that word. Joshua was a meditator.

As a result, God exalted Joshua in the sight of all Israel. The Lord was with him; He fought for him, even turning back the world's calendar for a whole day to ensure victory. For his part, Joshua obeyed God fully and took the whole land. And the land had rest from war. Not one of the good promises that the Lord had given failed. They all came to pass. The people of Israel served the Lord with their whole hearts throughout the lifetime of Joshua. He passed on the legacy of the Word to the extent that the people continued to follow the Lord fully even after his death.

Is this not spiritual warfare at its highest? Israel was not only fighting against flesh and blood but also against world forces of darkness and spiritual forces of wickedness in the heavenly places, as Paul later would remind the Ephesian Church. (Ephesians 6:20) Take note, then, of the powerful weapon given to Joshua by the Spirit of God: the Word of God. And as Judy Smith often says as she teaches the Book of Acts, "absolutely nothing can stop the Word of God!"[5]

Yes, Joshua was a strong warrior, a mighty conqueror. But what was the secret of his strength? We must leap ahead many centuries to hear the Apostle John describe the source of Joshua's great strength. John reveals that strength by saying, " . . . you are strong, and the Word of God abides in you, and you have overcome the evil one." (1 John 2:14b) Why was Joshua strong? Because the Word of God made its home in him. Joshua was a meditator; he allowed the Word of Christ to abide fully and abundantly in Him. Therefore he was strong. Therefore he was able to overcome the Evil One and take possession of the Promised Land.

Joshua was a meditator first, and then a conqueror, a possessor of nations who clung to the Word of the Lord until he himself was possessed by the Lord of all nations. Through meditation Joshua was freed from fear and negative expectations to become a man of faith whom Satan himself could not stop. His inner potential for greatness in leadership unlocked, he began to grow in wisdom and influence. With his mind focused only on the Lord, he was able to serve Him and his generation with singleness of mind and purity of heart.

God is searching today for men and women who will follow in Joshua's footsteps—men and women of the Word, young and old, who will allow the Spirit of God to reshape them through that Word so that they, too, may become possessors of nations for the glory of God.

Invitation to the Banquet Table
Personal Meditation on Psalm 139

1. Review the four simple steps of meditation.
First, prepare your heart.
Second, listen to all God wants to say to you through the text.
Third, seek to meet God as He reveals Himself to you.
Fourth, respond to Him in prayer and obedience

2. Read through the entire chapter of Psalm 139.
Open yourself to God and listen as you read.
Try to understand what the psalmist wants to express through this psalm.

3. Meditate on Psalm 139, **verse 15.**
My frame was not hidden from You,
When I was being made in secret,
Intricately woven in the depths of the earth.
Consider the loving care of your heavenly Father when He created you.
Ask God if He would like to tell you any secrets about how He made you.
Listen to what He wants to say to you personally!

4. Write down in your Meditation Journal what the Lord says to you.
Or you may write out your prayer to Him.
Allow the Spirit to lead you as you listen to the Lord.

5. Take time now to *wait upon the Lord.*
Give Him your heart. Ask Him to reveal Himself to you.

6. Spend time in prayer.
Thank God for His word to you.
Commit yourself to obey Him.

Chapter Thirteen

The Fruitful Word

> "He is like a tree planted by water,
> that . . . does not cease to bear fruit."
> Jeremiah 17:8

B ecoming a "possessor of nations," as Joshua was, is another way of saying that the believer is bearing fruit for the Lord. Fruitfulness is the great promise to the Christian who abides in Christ. "Whoever abides in Me and I in him, he it is that bears much fruit," declared Jesus to His disciples. (John 15:5) Fruit comes from abiding in Christ. It is in the bearing of much fruit that we Christians attain our highest joy because of two reasons: First, it glorifies God. Second, it is the evidence that we are Christ's disciples. (John 15:8)

But how is the believer to bear fruit? What must we do? The psalmist provides the answer. Psalm 1 contrasts the life and ultimate destiny of the righteous person, who seeks to live a godly life, with the unrighteous person, who mocks God. What is the key mark of the godly person who seeks to glorify God in all that he does? He is a *meditator* on the Word of God! "His delight is in the law of the Lord, and on

His law he meditates day and night . . . he is like a tree . . . that yields its fruit in its season." (Psalm 1:2-3) Meditation on the Word of God is the most important key for bearing fruit, because as we meditate, God's Word brings us into intimate fellowship with God, who then produces His fruit in and through our lives.

What assurance this brings to the believer in Christ! We are promised that if we will make our home in His Word, daily listening and responding to Christ as He speaks to us, we will bear fruit for the Lord! Not just workers for the Lord, not mere "project managers" for the affairs of God. No, the promise is that we will be *full partners* with Christ for the extension of His Kingdom! Our lives will reflect the image of Christ in a fallen world. Our words of witness to our Lord will be spoken with the authority of His Spirit. The "fragrance" of the Lord in us will draw unbelievers to the Lord, so that they also can receive new life and become His agents for change in the world. Is this not what the psalmist means when he promises that we will "yield fruit in season?"

The Secret of David's Heart

What kind of man was David, who was the chief representative of the psalmists? It is not likely that David wrote this first psalm, but most of the psalms reflect his heart, which is evident in this great promise of fruitfulness. We know him as a shepherd who communed with the Lord while tending his flock on the Judean hillsides. We honor him as one of the greatest worshipers of Israel, who was able to play music that would quiet Saul's restless spirit when evil spirits assailed him. We meet him throughout the Scriptures as a mighty warrior, a remarkable leader, a powerful king. Surely few people in history have been used in nation building to the extent that God used David. God Himself was pleased with David, saying, "I have found in David the son of Jesse a man after my heart, who will do all my will." (Acts 13:22)

What then was the secret of David's heart? He was a meditator! His heart was completely focused on the Lord. He later confessed, "I have set the Lord always before me; because He is at my right hand, I shall not be shaken." (Psalm 16:8) His lifestyle was that of a meditator: he walked in the presence of the Lord, inviting Him into all areas of his life. He listened constantly to the voice of the Lord and allowed that Word to break, cleanse, feed, remold and empower him. He was ready to repent and seek restoration from the Lord after he had sinned. He was quick to obey all that the Lord spoke to him, wholeheartedly committed to finish the work that the Lord gave him to do. The Lord knew that David would complete whatever task He committed to him to accomplish. But is this not true of all meditators? Why not ask the Lord now to speak to you, as you wait upon Him in full surrender, yielded to His will? Listen to Him say to you, just as He spoke to David, *"I have found in you a person after my heart, who will do all my will!"*

The Bible Is the Source of Meditation.

Meditation on the Word of God is so important that it is the theme of the very first psalm. The psalmist describes the blessed person as one who delights in the law of God and meditates on that law day and night. We may consider the phrase "law of God" used here as a synonym for "the whole Word of God."[1] He does not say, blessed is the one who listens to or studies the Word of God, or who memorizes the Word of God. Even though all of these are extremely important, the psalmist tells us that the *meditator* on the Word of God is the one who is blessed!

The Bible, God's written Word, must be the source of the Christian's meditation. True spirituality never departs from the Word of God. God's Holy Spirit always works through God's Word! "But the anointing—the Holy Spirit—that you received from Him abides in you and . . . teaches you about everything . . . abide in Him!" (1 John 2:27) We abide in the Spirit by abiding in God's Word. The deeper our spirituality, the deeper will be our abiding in the Word of God.

Abstract meditation with no object has no place in Christian spirituality. Christian meditation, as well as contemplation, always has a subject, and that subject is God Himself. But God reveals Himself to us most clearly and authoritatively in His Word. Even when the believer meditates on God Himself, or on His majesty in creation, or on the work that He has accomplished for us through the blood of His Son, still that meditation is nourished and enriched by God's written Word, the Bible.

We meditate on the Word of God by *storing in our hearts* the words that God speaks to us. As we meditate we *hide* the Word in our inner beings like a treasure, and we continually ponder and reflect on it just as Jesus' mother, Mary, did when the shepherds and Magi spoke mysteries to her. We prayerfully come before *each word* and ask God to speak deeply into our souls.[2]

Three Conditions for the Meditator

The first Psalm reveals the sharp contrast between the life of the righteous and the unrighteous. The unrighteous, or "wicked" person in the psalms is not just one who does evil deeds, but one who lives as if God did not exist, evading His love and ignoring and even "scoffing" at His commands. In contrast, the life of the righteous person is marked by a devotion to God's Word. The righteous person is the meditator!

The psalmist gives here three conditions for the meditator:

238

- A willingness to turn away from sin,
- A heart that delights in the Word of God and
- A determination to meditate on a daily basis. Let us examine these three conditions.

Turning Away From Sin

He begins with the primary condition for becoming a meditator. The meditator's life focus must be on God and obedience to His Word, not on the temporary pleasures of sin. "Blessed is the man who walks not in the counsel of the wicked, nor stands in the way of sinners, nor sits in the seat of scoffers." (Psalm 1:1) No one knew better than the psalmist that one cannot serve God and Satan at the same time. To be a meditator, we must choose between a self-centered life and a God-centered life. While it is true that a Christian is one who has been set free from the rule and power of sin by the Cross of Jesus Christ, nevertheless not even the most faithful meditator is completely free from sin. We have been crucified with Christ, yet we must continue to put to death the sinful deeds of the flesh. We have died but we must *continue* to die. As we do so, the direction of our lives will be moving away from sin and towards God. Then God will be highly pleased to "awaken our ears" each morning, so that we can listen as a disciple.

We must be aware, therefore, of the deceptiveness of sin. Notice the verbs in Psalm 1:1: *walk, stand, sit.* The unsuspecting believer begins by occasional compliance — *walking* into the midst of people who despise God and His Word, placing himself in a position to hear their opinions and judgments. Unaware of the snare that the Enemy has prepared for him, he lingers and *stands* among them, *associating* with them. Even though he may stand there out of curiosity, he already has placed himself in a vulnerable position. Finally, he identifies — *sits* among them and agrees with them.[3]

Without being aware of the power of the Enemy, he becomes entrapped in a lifestyle that he never desired. He may even begin to wonder why he is so confused and susceptible to the temptations of the flesh, the world and the devil.

How can a young, growing Christian keep his way pure? "By guarding it according to [God's] Word," answers the psalmist. (Psalm 119:9) He goes on to say, "I have stored up Your word in my heart, that I might not sin against You. (Psalm 119:11) Herein is the first condition for the meditator: turning away from sin, avoiding situations that would cause him to fall into temptation, and instead, turning to God with a listening heart, seeking joy in obedience to God rather than to Satan.

Delighting In the Word

Could anyone have taken more delight in hearing God speak than John the Baptist? John was a meditator on the words of the prophets, who spoke about the coming Messiah. Surely John pondered deeply *each word* of Isaiah, of Micah, of Moses, when they foretold the Messiah's birth and appearance. We can imagine the long hours that John spent meditating on the words of the prophets, line-by-line, word-by-word, filled with an insatiable desire to know experientially all that God was revealing about His Son, Jesus. Then when Jesus the Messiah actually appeared, he described himself as a "friend" of the Bridegroom whose greatest joy was listening to the voice of the Bridegroom! "The friend of the bridegroom, who stands and hears him, rejoices greatly at the bridegroom's voice. Therefore this joy of mine is now complete!" (John 3:29)

Surely the need to rejoice is one of mankind's basic needs. Without joy, our sorrow would be overwhelming and unbearable. "In life, sorrow tends to last just a little longer than joy. So we try to just touch the joy to alleviate the sorrow." So spoke Abdul Razak Al-Alawi, a founder and conductor of the Iraqi National Symphony Orchestra.

God wants us to "touch His joy," even in the midst of great tragedy such as the nation of Iraq has endured and still endures. But He wants to give us more. He desires us to know the heights of His joy over us. "As the bridegroom rejoices over the bride, so shall your God rejoice over you," says the prophet Isaiah. (Isaiah 62:5) But Zephaniah the prophet stated it most beautifully: "The Lord your God is in your midst, a mighty one who will save; He will rejoice over you with gladness; He will quiet you by His love; He will exult over you with loud singing." (Zephaniah 3:17) The Spirit of God seeks to flood the believer's soul with the wondrous joy of the Lord. Were not the believers overcome with joy at Pentecost, when the Spirit came upon them in power and they were immersed in the Holy Spirit? Even persecution could not take away that joy! C. S. Lewis would say they were "surprised by joy!"

But how are we to maintain this joy, to walk in fullness of joy in the presence of the Lord? Only by abiding in the Word of God! "These things I have spoken to you," said Jesus, "that my joy may be in you, and that your joy may be full." (John 15:11) Jesus continues to speak to us today in His Word.

Of course He speaks to us in innumerable ways, but none can compare with His words through which He continues to speak to us in the Holy Scriptures. Christians constantly need to be reminded that there is no authentic spirituality that bypasses, or attempts to go beyond, the written Word of God. No one can express this truth better than the psalmist, who confessed, "Your testimonies are my heritage forever, for they are the joy of my heart!" (Psalm 119:111)

There is a cost to maintaining this joy, as Jesus revealed when He told a parable about a man who found a treasure. "The kingdom of heaven is like treasure hidden in a field, which a man found and covered up." (Matthew 13:44) The man was so delighted in what he found that he went home and sold all his possessions and bought the field! The riches and possessions that he already owned were of no value to him, compared to the treasure that he wanted to possess.

Many are those who would give up smaller material possessions to gain greater ones. But Jesus is speaking about *spiritual* treasures. There are things we must give up in order to enjoy the deeper life of joy and power in God. When we confess that our greatest joy in life is to hear God speak, to listen to His voice and abide in that Word, we are saying that we are willing to give up lesser things that demand our time and energies. We are committing ourselves to a disciplined life. But the rewards are great!

Determining to Meditate As a Daily Discipline

God's mercy and grace come to us daily, not just once in a lifetime or on special occasions. His mercies never come to an end; they are new every morning! (Lamentations 3:23) So also the Christian's response to God's love must be a daily committing of our lives to be used by Him as He desires. "If anyone would come after me, let him deny himself and take up his cross *daily* and follow me," said Jesus. (Luke 9:23) Spiritual discipline, like God's grace, is a daily affair.

Meditation on the Word of God as a spiritual discipline must be done on a daily basis, insofar as possible. For this reason, the psalmist echoes the words of Joshua, when he says that the meditator on God's Word meditates *day and night.*" (Psalm 1:2, Joshua 1:8). Both men were involved in nation building, and both knew that the key to building a godly nation was its citizens meditating on God's words daily, tuning their ears to hear all that He would say to them, with hearts and wills ready to obey! The third condition to become a meditator, then, is to make a decision to meditate on a daily basis.

What does it mean to meditate *day and night?* The obvious meaning is to meditate on a Word from Scripture in the morning, perhaps the most important time in the believer's daily schedule, and again in the evening, another key time for the Christian. As the Lord opens our ears each morning to listen as a disciple, He opens the door for us to hear His vision for that day and then to walk with Him throughout the day in faith. In the evening the Lord then opens the door for us receive His peace and serenity as He sends His angels to watch over us throughout the sleeping hours.

The psalmist speaks often about remaining awake during the watches of the night to hear the Lord speak, or of arising early before dawn to listen to the voice of the Lord. One Christian doctor prescribes Bible meditation for his patients just as he would medicine: one pill in the morning upon arising, one at night before retiring, one verse in the morning, one at night. And he testifies to the results, both physical and spiritual!

Another meaning of meditating *day and night* is to meditate *continually,* that is, with regularity, on a daily basis. Ellen and I realized early in our ministry that daily meditation on the Word of God was one of the key secrets of all ministry. Many are the things that we should do, or that are good to do. But the one *essential* thing is to abide in the Word of Christ on a daily basis, and this can be done best through meditation and prayer. We saw the direct effects in our own lives and ministry: a deepening of our spiritual relationship with the Lord, intimacy with Him and great joy in His presence, healing and restoration of our emotions, a new keenness in intellectually understanding God and His ways, and even renewed strength physically. Long years ago, the Lord spoke to me and told me that two keys to continuing health were daily meditation on the Word of God to strengthen my spirit, and daily physical exercise to strengthen my body!

Meditation has proven to be a tool that has enabled me to grow as a Christian—not the *only* key, but certainly an important one. Both Ellen and I have meditated regularly on the Bible for over thirty-five years. Our excitement about Bible meditation began when we were baptized in the Holy Spirit in 1972 and continues to increase. God revealed to us during those days and months when we were first longing for a deeper walk in His Spirit, that we must abide in the Anointing (the Holy Spirit) who abides in us and who teaches us all things. We saw and experienced that the Spirit always leads His people into God's Word! And we can bear testimony of the transformation that comes from abiding in God's Word.

But I can bear witness also to the dangers of *not abiding daily* in God's Word. There have been days, even weeks, when I have neglected to abide in God's Word. Those times, when I did not daily enter into the "council of the Lord,"[4] were times of spiritual barrenness: spiritual weakness through suffering loss of intimacy with the Lord; and moral weakness by becoming more easily susceptible to Satan's temptations and attacks, not only on myself but also on my family and ministry. There have been times when I tended to produce "works" for the Lord rather than allowing the Lord to produce His fruit through me.

What then is the danger of not meditating daily on the Word of God? It is not that we will become "second-class Christians," or that God will punish us for disobeying revealed truth. No, the danger is greater than that: it is that we will then meditate on *other things that are not allowed by God as objects of meditation!* These things usually will produce in us negative or immoral results. Remember, dear reader, that Satan is always waiting to fill any gap that occurs in our lives, spiritually, intellectually or emotionally, with his destructive substitutes.

The truth about us as humans is that God created us to be meditators! He placed the great mystery of Himself deep within our spirits. He endowed us with imagination and the ability to focus on Him and to be filled with joy in His presence. When we neglect to meditate on God, by nature we still constantly seek to fix our thoughts and the direction of our hearts on some other object. And we gradually become like the object of our meditation. Young people may fill the gap by filling their minds and hearts with destructive forms of music whose words lead them to commit violence against either themselves or others, or through being preoccupied with violent video games. Many adult Christians meditate on *mammon*, on the materialistic pleasures of life, and fill their hearts and minds with what they can possess. Still others set their hearts on pleasures through improper relationships. King David meditated on and filled his heart with a person, Bathsheba, as he pondered, mused and fantasized over her beauty. He may have "meditated" on her for only a few moments, but the results lasted much longer. His meditation led him to commit the sins of adultery and murder, bringing great harm to Bathsheba and to himself and nearly destroying the kingdom!

Yes, a basic principle of meditation is that we become like the object of our meditation. Young people who meditate on destructive lyrics of songs and on violent video games may be more prone to suicide and acts of violence than those who do not. People who focus their lives on money and possessions are less likely to be compassionate and generous to those in need. Those who fantasize about sex and immoral relations will often at some time engage in those improper activities.

We are all meditators; we have been so since birth. We were created by God to meditate on His wonders, on His holiness and awesome beauty. If we do not meditate on God, we will meditate on something else, and those things will shape our lives! God does not tell us that we must become meditators. W*e already are!* Instead, He tells us to *change the object* of our meditation, from Satan and the things of the world—the desires of the flesh and the desires of the eyes and pride in possessions, all these things that are passing away—and to redirect our thoughts and focus all our being on *God Himself!* (1 John 2:15-16) The psalmist declares: "Let the words of my mouth and the meditation of my heart be acceptable in your sight, O Lord, my rock and my redeemer!" (Psalm 19:14)

As we actually meditate *day and night,* allowing God to awaken our ear in the morning so that we can listen as His disciple, and then committing ourselves to Him in the evening before we sleep, we begin to develop a lifestyle of continual, daily meditation. Then we discover that God is preparing us for an even deeper understanding of what it means to meditate *day and night:* He will allow us to meditate *continuously,* in unbroken communion with Him, never being away from His presence but rather *practicing the presence of the Lord,* as Brother Lawrence demonstrated. The word that the Lord speaks to us in the early morning will remain with us throughout the day, planted deeply in our spirits by God's Spirit. As the Spirit causes us to think again about that word, to ponder and reflect on it as we go about our daily chores and schedule, we come to understand that God's Word never leaves us! It takes up its abode within us and abides abundantly in us. At that point we will discover that we not only have *times of solitude* but rather that our life itself gradually becomes a *life of solitude,* of walking with the Lord in all of our daily affairs.

The Fruitfulness of the Meditator

Ever-present fellowship, ever-present renewal! Is this not the context of the life that never ceases to bear fruit, that never fears "when heat comes," nor is anxious in the year of drought? (Jeremiah 17:7-8) Who could begin to measure the fruitfulness of the life of a meditator on the Word of God? We have seen that God *desires* us to bear fruit and is pleased when we bear much fruit. We understand now, also, that meditation on the Word of God *guarantees* that the believer will bear fruit for the Lord.

How amazing that the very conditions for becoming a meditator—turning away from sin, rejoicing in God and His Word, determining to meditate on a daily basis— actually become the *fruit* of meditation! The meditator, filled with inexpressible joy in God and in hearing His voice, finds deep resources within himself to resist Satan's attacks and temptations. Moreover he becomes increasingly aware of God's presence that never leaves him, even in times of trial and distress. Through daily meditation he discovers that the foundation of all blessings is the presence of the Lord, which he has entered more fully through the portals of God's Word! *The meditator is aware that God is always present with His people, but he knows with certainty that he becomes more aware of that Presence as he meditates on God's Word.* As he meditates, he increasingly yields his whole life to God, to be available to Him for His great purposes in the world. Then he understands Jesus' words to His disciples, "If you abide in Me, and My words abide in you, ask whatever you wish, and it will be done for you." (John 15:7) The joy of intimacy with the Lord, constantly available strength to overcome the Enemy, the promise of unlimited ministry—could we ask for greater blessings as we seek to live our lives for the glory of the Lord?

Stability

The psalmist describes the meditator as "a tree planted by streams of water." (Psalm 1:3) The prophet Isaiah refers to God's people, through whom God chooses to reveal His glory, as "oaks of righteousness," or "the planting of the Lord that He may be glorified." (Isaiah 61:3) The meditator on God's Word becomes a person of great stability, emotionally as well as spiritually, a strong member of his community. He is deeply rooted in the soil of God's unchanging Word and in the deep waters of His Holy Spirit. The storms of life may assail him, but he will continue to stand.

King Sejong the Great (1397-1450), who invented the Korean alphabet—*hangul*—and in whose honor the International Phonetic Society is named (The Sejong Society), understood the importance of stability. He wrote,

> *The tree whose roots deeply penetrate the earth*
> *Will not fall when swayed by fierce wind.*
> *Beautiful will be its flowering, abundant its fruit.*
>
> *The well that draws from deeply imbedded springs*
> *Never runs dry in seasons of drought . . .*
> *Its waters fill the streams that flow into the sea.*[5]

How amazing that long before missionaries brought the Christian Gospel to Korea, God Himself planted the seeds of that Gospel in the hearts of His people there! God sent His *missionary Word* to the land of Korea even before He sent His missionary people! As missiologists continue to explore the reasons for the great success of the Christian Gospel in Korea they cannot overlook the fact that God "planted eternity" within the hearts of His people there long before the Gospel actually arrived! (Ecclesiastes 3:11) He gave them a heart to seek after Him and to eagerly desire His Word. Perhaps King Sejong would have been a fervent disciple of Jesus Christ, had he the opportunity to have met Him!

This explains, partially, the centrality of the Word of God in the Korean Church. But this is also a call to

Christians worldwide. Those who meditate on that Word will become persons of great stability whom God can use as He empowers His Church to become a missionary Church, committed to world evangelization.

Guaranteed Fruitfulness

Isaiah, speaking of the surviving remnant of the house of Judah, says that they will "take root downward and bear fruit upward!" (Isaiah 37:31) Such is the life of the meditator. As we abide in Jesus, and in His Word, the Lord Himself guarantees fruitfulness! (John 15:5, Psalm 1:3)

Fruitfulness is not the work we do for the Lord, nor the projects and programs we plan for Him. It is not even the great organizations or churches we build for Him. No, fruitfulness is the Lord Himself working through us to extend His Kingdom. It is the Spirit of God remolding the image of Christ within us so that the world will see us and turn to the Lord. Fruitfulness is the Spirit's re-forming Christ in us so that the knowledge of the Lord will cover the earth as the waters cover the sea. This fruitfulness does not depend on outward circumstances. On the contrary, the persecuted "Suffering Church" often bears more fruit than churches that are recognized and honored by human authorities. David himself, the author of many of the psalms, continued to bear fruit even while he endured persecution at the hands of Saul. Two of the most beautiful poems ever composed—Psalm 34, composed when David was forced to feign madness before King Abimelech when he was trying to escape King Saul's madness, and Psalm 63, composed while David hid among the caves of the wilderness of Judea—bear witness to great fruitfulness even in times of terrible suffering. This life of fruitfulness is a promise to everyone who meditates on the Word of God!

Constant Freshness

"He is like a tree . . . and its leaf does not wither." (Psalm 1:3) The meditator's life retains a freshness that attracts rather than repels others. Freshness of spirit knows no age; it is a sign of a youthful spirit continually renewed by the Spirit working through His Word. Consider the beauty of elderly saints who have spent their lives abiding in God's Word, walking with the Lord often in times of great suffering and tragedy. Their bodies become weakened and dependent on others, yet their spirits retain a vitality and freshness that encourages and strengthens others. By contrast, a person may possess the physical beauty of youth while slowly decaying within. Rather than refreshing others, his joyless spirit brings sadness and tiredness to those around him.

The difference lies in whom we place our trust. The meditator enters daily into the throne room of heaven, there to meet His Savior and Friend and to place himself in His hands. He remains there in the presence of the Lord and is renewed and filled with joy in His presence; he has a listening heart, eagerly seeking to hear His Master's voice so that he can obey His will. By contrast, the one who does not meet God daily in His Word has only himself to trust in, and has no word to give the weary traveler who stops by his doorstep for comfort and help. He is like a "shrub in the desert," says Jeremiah, "and shall not see any good come. He shall dwell in the parched places of the wilderness." (Jeremiah 17:5-6)

But Jeremiah continues. "Blessed is the man who trusts in the Lord, whose *trust is the Lord*. He is like a tree planted by water . . . and does not fear when heat comes, for its *leaves remain green,* and is not anxious in the year of drought, for it does not cease to bear fruit. (Jeremiah 17:7-8) *Green leaves in drought!* Always fresh, even in the midst of suffering or adversity, able to strengthen the community of which he is a part. This is the blessing of the meditator on God's Word.

This is why Caleb, when he was an old man, could say that his strength then was the same as when he was young, and could claim his inheritance in the Promised Land.

Continuing Prosperity

The meditator is promised prosperity in all that he does! Yet we must not be deceived into thinking that when we meditate on the Word of God all our financial woes will disappear and we will become wealthy with no physical ailments. No, the meditator, like all others, lives in a sinful world and suffers along with the rest.

What does prosperity mean for the Christian? Isaiah gave the best answer when he described Jesus Christ, the Suffering Servant, who would be crushed with grief as He poured out His life as an offering for sin. Yet, Isaiah says, "the will of the Lord *shall prosper in his hand!"* (Isaiah 53:10) Biblical prosperity means that *God's will prospers through our lives,* as we walk in submission to Him and share His sacrificial love for the world. Yet God promises to supply all of our needs when we desire to see *His* will prosper rather than our own. "Great is the Lord, who delights in the welfare of His servant!" (Psalm 35:27)

Known By God

"For the Lord knows the way of the righteous," proclaims the psalmist as he closes the first psalm. God acknowledges the meditator as one of His own, His servant who will do all that He tells him to do. He watches over his way, so that he does not need to seek the approval of men. Try to imagine, dear reader, what your life would be if you lived it with the awareness that God Himself knows you completely and approves of you, that He recognizes the righteousness of His own Son Jesus as being your righteousness, and acknowledges and loves you as His servant! What freedom you would have, to please God alone and no one else! Indeed this is the freedom of the meditator. One who meditates day and night on the Word of God *already* is approved by the One who awakens him each morning and who speaks to him throughout the day.

Psalm 1 does not tell the complete story of the fruitfulness of the meditator. Probably no book could contain the innumerable blessings that come to those who abide in Jesus—God's Word incarnate—and in His words found in the Bible. But as we meditate we come to know that we are being transformed daily into the image of God's Son, Jesus. We gradually become renewed in our thinking so that we begin to think biblically, as God thinks. Our will becomes redirected so that our only desire is to please our Father and commit ourselves to Him for the extension of His Kingdom. Our emotions become healed so that we become God's instruments to heal a broken world. We begin to develop the mind of Christ. Surely *His will begins to prosper through our lives!*

Invitation to the Banquet Table
Personal Meditation on Psalm 139

1. Review the four simple steps of meditation.
First, prepare your heart.
Second, listen to all God wants to say to you through the text.
Third, seek to meet God as He reveals Himself to you.
Fourth, respond to Him in prayer and obedience.

2. Read through the entire chapter of Psalm 139.
Open yourself to God and listen as you read.
Try to understand what the psalmist wants to express through this psalm.

3. Meditate on Psalm 139, **verse 16.**
Your eyes saw my unformed substance;
In your book were written, every one of them,
The days that were formed for me,
When as yet there were none of them.
Your times are in God's hands. He has a plan for your life that is perfect.
He desires to speak with you about His plan for your life.
Listen to what the Lord wants to say to you personally!

4. Write down in your Meditation Journal what the Lord
says to you.
Or you may write out your prayer to Him.
Allow the Spirit to lead you as you listen to the Lord.

5. Take time now to *wait upon the Lord*.
Give Him your heart. Ask Him to reveal Himself to you.

6. Spend time in prayer.
Thank God for His word to you.
Commit yourself to obey Him.

Part Four

The Act of Meditation

The Spirit of God, who reveals the Word of
God to us
and remolds us through that Word,
has given us the
power to meditate on that Word
so that it may perform its work within us.

As we begin our journey
of meditating on God's Word,
here are some tools to aid us on our way.

As we become familiar with
these aids to meditation,
we will be ready to embark on that journey
that leads into the heart of God.

Chapter Fourteen

Tools for Meditation

"Let Your hand be ready to help me,
for I have chosen Your precepts."
Psalm 119:173

God has provided us with tools to aid us as we meditate. We will explore six of those tools: observation, understanding, repetition, memory, imagination and soliloquy.

The First Tool: Observation

"He *sees* many things," says the Lord, referring to Israel's failure to see and hear Him, "but does not *observe* them." (Isaiah 42:20) How true this is, not only in Bible study and meditation, but also in our everyday life. Have you not walked along the same street for many years and yet one day discovered something that you had never before seen? It was always there, but you had never focused your attention on it or even noticed that it was there. Good friends, even married couples, sometimes newly discover beautiful things about one another that they had never before observed.

How much more true this is of the Scriptures. Observation is the key not only to meditation but also to all Bible study. How do we observe when meditating? By asking simple questions that can be answered by observing the content of the text. The questions are: Who? Did or said what? To whom? When? Where? Why? How? With what results?

All of these questions can be answered simply by observing what the text says. Meditation then becomes more meaningful, because we are meditating on the actual words and ideas of the text rather than on some preconceived idea of our own.

A good rule of thumb to follow when you meditate: Keep your eyes open so you can *see* the actual words of the verse. Think about each word; say it over to yourself until you understand what the author is actually saying. Then as you listen to the Lord who desires to speak to you through that Word, you can close your eyes and focus on Him and pray that His will may be accomplished in your life through your meditation.

George MacDonald tells the story of the transformation of a young man named Adam who was frail in body and also dull in spirit. Unaware of people and things surrounding him, not noticing the beauty and uniqueness of his own community, he lived an isolated life. But then he learned to *observe* the people and other events around him, and his life was totally changed. MacDonald writes:

> *The growth of Adam's observation was remarkable. The number of events and circumstances he was able to see by the end of the month, compared with what he had seen in the beginning, was wonderful . . . So at length the youth who had walked along Cheapside village without seeing that one face differed from another, now knew most of the birds and*

> *many of the insects, and could in general*
> *tell what they were about. He delighted in*
> *the grass and wild flowers, the sky and the*
> *clouds and the stars, and knew, in a real, vital*
> *way, about the world in which he lived. He*
> *entered into the life that was going on about*
> *him, and so in the house of God became one*
> *of the family. He had ten times his former*
> *consciousness; his life was ten times the size*
> *it was before. As was natural, his health had*
> *improved marvelously. For there is nothing*
> *like interest in life to quicken the body's vital*
> *forces.*[1]

Observation changes our outlook on all of life. It is the secret of all study, and it is essential for the creative arts and relationships. West Fraser, one of the leading landscape artists of the southeastern United States, remarked, "I use what I'm looking at. I react and observe." Observation will enable you to become an effective and fruitful meditator.

The Second Tool: Understanding

We have spoken of the integral relationship between meditation and study. We must understand the Scripture on which we meditate; otherwise our meditation will be meaningless. It is true of course that we cannot understand a text *fully* until we have meditated on it, but we still must seek to understand with our minds so that we can embrace the truth with our hearts and respond with our wills.

When we meditate verse-by-verse, word-by-word, through a passage of Scripture, it is important to first read through the entire passage *before* beginning to meditate. For example, if you were to choose Paul's letter to the Philippian Christians as the book on which you plan to meditate, the first thing you should do is to read through the entire letter aloud at one sitting. Seek to understand what Paul is saying to the Philippian Christians. What is their situation? Why is he writing? How does he exhort them, or comfort them? What is the main idea of the letter? After doing that you would begin meditating in the first chapter, verse one.

Each day, before you begin your meditation, it would be good to read through the entire chapter or unit of thought and once again seek to understand the meaning of that chapter, or the individual paragraphs. Then as you meditate on each verse, you will understand what God is saying to you and your meditation will be enriched.

Some people teach that we must first "empty" our minds of all previously attained knowledge about the verse or verses on which we are meditating. On the contrary, the opposite is true. All Bible knowledge that we have previously acquired will enrich our meditation. Union with Christ begins with seeking to know Him with our minds. When God speaks, His word comes first to our minds, then through our minds to our spirit and will. The mind is not in conflict with the spirit; rather it is the vehicle by which we receive God's words.

Often as you meditate you will remember another passage that is related to the one on which you are focusing. Take time to look up the other Scripture, read it and seek to understand it. If you use a cross-reference Bible, you will be able to find similar passages or verses that will aid your understanding. This is not an interruption to your meditation, but rather a help. The more you understand the whole Counsel of God, the more your meditation will be enriched.

The Third Tool: Repetition

There is a repetition that is tiring, but there also is a repetition that brings peace and calm to the spirit. Many believers are not accustomed to repetition; at least they think they are not, unless they consider how often they repeat themselves in an ordinary, everyday conversation. Who has not been made weary by a friend who constantly repeats the same idea, even the same words, over and over in a conversation? Or consider the verbose politician who repeats himself endlessly while trying to convince an audience of the importance of his ideas. Many churches that disdain liturgy nevertheless have their own "hidden liturgy." They would never dare change their order of worship even though they vigorously deny that they have a set order! Such repetition may be tiring.

But there is repetition that is refreshing and calming to our spirits. We can find this in corporate confession of the Creeds of the Church, or in the regular praying of the Lord's Prayer. Those who worship in liturgical churches benefit from repetition of prayers and confessions that have been passed down in the Church's tradition for many hundreds of years, tried and tested throughout the centuries by the cloud of witnesses who have gone before us. Repetitive but not tiring.

One of the most beautiful places to experience the beauty of repetition in singing and worship is in the Taizé Community in France. Brother Roger founded the Taizé Community in 1940, in the early days of the Second World War. The son of a Protestant pastor, he was puzzled to observe his father go frequently to the local Roman Catholic church to pray. When he asked his father why he went, he replied that he went to pray for reconciliation between divided Christians and separated peoples.

Brother Roger set out from his home in Switzerland at the age of twenty-five, to look for a place to create a community of reconciliation, where simplicity and kindheartedness could be lived out. He arrived in a small French village and asked an elderly woman where he could buy food. "There is no place to buy food in our village," she told him, but she invited him into her home for a meal. When he told the elderly couple his vision, they begged him to stay there. "We are poor and lonely, please stay with us," she pleaded. So Brother Roger made the decision to begin his community there, in the village of Taizé, France.

Today over one hundred brothers, Catholics and Protestants, make up the Taizé Community, with thousands of pilgrims visiting annually. They are noted for the beauty of their singing. Their songs are usually very brief and simple, often consisting of only one line. The following is the way the community describes their singing:

> *Singing is one of the most essential elements of worship. Short songs, repeated again and again, give it a meditative character. Using just a few words they express a basic reality of faith, quickly grasped by the mind. As the words are sung over many times, this reality gradually penetrates the whole being. Meditative singing thus becomes a way of listening to God. It allows everyone to take part in a time of prayer together and to remain together in attentive waiting on God.*[2]

Their CD entitled *Venite Exultemus* contains some excellent examples of this repetition.[3] The chorus of one song is: "The soul filled by love neither tires others nor grows tired." Imagine singing this over and over as the Spirit of God renews and refreshes the singers in mind and body. Or those who sing, "Look to God and you will shine, all bitterness gone from your face," will be transformed as they sing these simple words while directing their thoughts and hearts toward the Lord. Other songs create faith and willingness to commit to the Lord, such as, "God is nothing but love. Dare to give all for love. God is nothing but love. Give yourselves without fear."

The most powerful and potentially life-changing song, however, may be the *"Kyrie Eleison,"* which simply means, "Lord, have mercy." This short song is actually Scripture, and is the basis for the "Jesus Prayer," which has been prayed over many centuries and is one of the oldest known prayers in existence. This is the prayer:

> *Lord Jesus Christ, Son of God,*
> *Have mercy on me, a sinner.*

Jesus told two stories that form the basis for this prayer. First, He told the story of a Pharisee and a tax collector who went up into the temple to pray. The Pharisee was hypocritical and proud, multiplying his words while exalting himself and looking down upon the tax collector. The tax collector, on the contrary, was so aware of his sin and unworthiness that he would not even look to heaven. His prayer was simple: "God, be merciful to me, a sinner." (Luke 18:9-14)

Jesus' second story was about a blind beggar, possibly Bartimaeus, who was desperate and single-minded in his desire to be healed by Jesus. His simple prayer was, "Jesus, Son of David, have mercy on me!" (Luke 18:35-43)

Christians of many nations and denominations have prayed the "Jesus Prayer" for at least seventeen centuries, and many have been healed, restored and empowered through repeating these simple words of Scripture. The prayer's power comes from its utter simplicity and from the repetition of God's own words.

I was scheduled to speak to a large audience on the subject of missions. Those gathered represented many different churches and organizations, and it was an important time to encourage and challenge God's people for the task of world evangelization. But just before I was to speak, my mind became filled with confusion and unrest, even though I was fully prepared. I prayed and God spoke assurance to me that He would use me as His vessel. Nevertheless my mind remained cluttered and I was unable to focus on the subject, suddenly struggling with feelings of unworthiness and inability. I began to pray the Jesus Prayer— *"Lord Jesus Christ, Son of God, have mercy on me, a sinner."* As I continued to repeat this prayer up to fifty times or more, a deep peace began to settle in my spirit, and Jesus spoke His words to me, "I can do all things through Him who strengthens me" (Philippians 4:13) I was praying Jesus' own words to Him, just as my ancestors in the faith had prayed for many centuries; and Jesus answered me with His own words of Scripture! And I became free to be used by God to speak to His people about His heart.

Repetition is a secret of meditation. A good way to begin meditation on a verse of Scripture is to repeat the verse aloud over and over, even fifteen or twenty times, before pausing to listen to the Spirit's speaking through the words. "The Lord is my shepherd; I shall not want." (Psalm 23:1) As you repeat this one sentence aloud you are making a great confession of faith, not just once but over and over again. You may not feel any strong emotion, but the word begins to enter your spirit. You will begin to experience the power that comes from the discipline of repetition, and the Holy Spirit will begin to plant the seed of the Word in your inner being. As you ponder the words of this psalm with your mind, while repeating them with your lips, you will begin to focus on Jesus, the Good Shepherd who provides all your needs. Then you can welcome the Shepherd *with your heart,* and begin to dwell in His presence.

Repetition is a God-given tool for our spiritual growth. As we worship, singing simple words of Scripture— *"Bless the Lord, O my soul, and all that is within me, bless his holy name"*—God will open the gates of heaven and allow us to enter into His presence. The secret is to *repeat* these words, not to add to them. Rather than adding new words such as, "Thank the Lord, O my soul," or "Serve the Lord, O my soul," we simply repeat the words of Scripture. As we do so, the power of the Lord will fall upon us. And we come to understand that worship very naturally flows out of meditation. This is why the brothers of the Taizé Community speak of *meditative singing*.

Experiment with the use of repetition as you meditate. Repeat over and over the verse on which you are meditating and allow God to quicken your spirit by His Spirit. Remember that repetition is a *tool* for meditating. Repetition in itself has no power to strengthen you. It is the Word that you are repeating that will encourage your soul.

The Fourth Tool: Memory

The use of memory is basic to living a normal life. Few things are as sad as families who cannot communicate with an older loved one because of memory loss. We take for granted the ability and capacity of the brain to store information and release it when required. If memory is basic to our life, then it must be true that it is basic to our relationship with God.[4]

We are commanded by God to remember His words and deeds, His covenant with His people. "You shall remember," declared God to the Israelites, "that you were a slave in the land of Egypt, and the Lord your God brought you out from there with a mighty hand and an outstretched arm." (Deuteronomy 5:15) Again He charges them:

> *You shall therefore lay up these words of mine in your heart and in your soul, and you shall bind them as a sign on your hand, and they shall be as frontlets between your eyes. You*

> *shall teach them to your children, talking of them when you are sitting in your house, and when you are walking by the way, and when you lie down, and when you rise. You shall write them on the doorposts of your house and on your gates, that your days and the days of your children may be multiplied in the land that the Lord swore to your fathers to give them.* (Deuteronomy 11:18-21)

Memory is the storehouse of God's words and deeds, and it becomes a rich resource of strength and power to live lives of continual praise and thanksgiving, giving God glory in all that we do. Surely, then, memorization of key Scripture passages is vitally important to maintaining the life of faith, as is the memorization of the basic creeds of the Church. This enables us to remember clearly what God has said, regarding His faithfulness in times of trial, and His commands that need to be obeyed. Memory of God's past faithfulness fills us with expectation for the future. One basic theme that runs throughout the Book of Psalms is *remembrance and expectation*—remembering how God has worked in the past, expecting Him to be true to His Word in the future.

To remember is to "re-experience." When we consider the works God has done in the past, we re-experience His goodness in the present. Re-experiencing leads to recommitment and obedience. One of Paul's last words to his young disciple Timothy was, "remember Jesus Christ." (2 Timothy 2:8) Paul was encouraging Timothy to "fan into flame" the gift of God which became his when Paul laid hands on him, so that he could be obedient to the end.

For Christians, the supreme act of memory is to partake of the Lord's Supper. Jesus took bread, and when He had given thanks he broke it and said, "This is My body which is for you. Do this *in remembrance* of Me. In the same way also he took the cup, after supper, saying, 'This cup is the new covenant in My blood. Do this, as often as you drink it, *in remembrance* of Me.'" (1 Corinthians 11:24-25) Partaking of the Lord's Supper is an act of meditation. We remember His great sacrifice for us. By remembering we re-experience His unlimited love. We enter into communion with our risen Lord and with other Christians with whom we partake. We meet Christ and are healed and renewed. Church history is filled with accounts of people who have been healed, restored, even delivered during this time of Holy Communion with the Lord. The result of this act of meditation and remembering is that we recommit ourselves to serving the King of Kings who, unlike false gods, stooped low enough to enter our suffering and deliver us from evil.

Memory is essential for meditation. The psalmist sometimes uses the two words synonymously, as in Psalm 77:6, "Let me remember my song in the night; let me meditate in my heart. Then my spirit made a diligent search." I once was meditating on the words "and my God will supply every need of yours according to His riches in glory in Christ Jesus." (Philippians 4:19) I continued to sit before the Lord with this one verse of Scripture, waiting for Him to speak. I knew that the reason Paul gave such a promise of God's boundless provision for the Philippian Christians was that they were a very generous church, giving of themselves and their money even beyond their ability. He was saying that God would honor their generosity by providing for all of their needs. Our ministry in Korea had been a generous ministry, helping many people. But at the very time I was meditating on this passage we were encountering a difficult time financially. Most of our nearly one hundred member Youth With A Mission staff were eating only barley instead of the white rice that we all liked, with very few appetizing side dishes. Yet here was Paul saying that God would liberally supply all of our needs. I admit that I was having trouble actually appropriating this promise.

Suddenly I remembered an incident that had happened a few years before. Thirty-four of our members were on an evangelistic trip that would take us around the whole nation of South Korea, beginning in Seoul, visiting the eastern mountain region of Taebaek, continuing on to Kwangju in the south then back to Seoul. But after ministering in our first destination our funds were already depleted. We had no money even for the bus trip back to Seoul. Standing around the large clock tower at the train station in Taebaek, we decided to pray and praise God for His faithfulness. We did not see the well-dressed man who approached one of the members of our team, but after he left and we had finished our time of praise, we opened the yellow envelope that he had given to the team member. "I am an elder of a church," he said, "but because of a problem I am not able to attend my church at the present time. When I heard your singing, though, I decided I would like to give you a small offering to bless you." The envelope contained enough money for our entire team to complete the trip, return to Seoul and still have enough money left over to make an offering to a local church! God is faithful indeed.

And that is the message I personally needed to hear while I meditated, now years later, on Philippians 4:19! I had entered into doubt because of circumstances, so God *caused me to remember* this instance of His grace during that former trip. This memory caused me to repent of my doubt, ask God's forgiveness and once again begin to trust Him that He would be faithful to His Word. Yes, He is faithful indeed!

The Fifth Tool: Imagination

"Imagination is more important than knowledge," wrote Albert Einstein. It is not enough to know a subject intellectually. We must use our imagination to apply that knowledge and to use it for creative purposes. Robots are increasingly becoming able to perform more human functions, and it is said that robots may eventually replace the computer. Recently a designer of the new generation of robots said: "The next generation of robots will be produced not by knowledge but by imagination!"

We must use our imagination to understand the Bible and God's dealings with man. Alister McGrath maintains that "Christian spirituality stresses the importance of an *imaginative encounter* (italics mine) with the crucified Christ in order to avoid abstract, impersonal, dehistoricized ways of thinking about the theological significance of [the Cross]." We must have a believing mind as we approach God's Word. But we also must have a believing *imagination*.[5]

"Only faith can prove the existence of realities that are unseen," says the author of the book of Hebrews.[6] Enoch is the first to be introduced in the eleventh chapter of Hebrews' great "Faith Hall of Fame." Enoch "walked with God." He saw God in a way other men and women of his age could never imagine. And God was pleased with him.

This well-known passage speaks of Abraham, who was not content to rest his gaze on the cities and places surrounding him but eagerly searched for that city which has foundations, whose architect and builder is God. Many others saw God through the eyes of faith and therefore were able to conquer kingdoms and transform weakness into faith. The first Christian martyr, Stephen, as he was being stoned to death for his faith, saw Jesus standing by the throne of the Father.

All these men and women of God were using their imaginations as tools from God to see Him who is unseen and to fix their eyes upon Him in order to walk with Him the life of faith.

The Apostle John "saw" the new heavens and the new earth, the New Jerusalem coming down out of heaven as a bride adorned for the Bridegroom. He "saw" the river of life flowing from the heavenly city, its banks flourishing with trees whose leaves brought healing to the nations.

In the Revelation John speaks of objects we know—a city, trees, a river—but his description of these objects is marked by a power that goes beyond the particulars of the things about which he is talking. This is the *power of sanctified imagination!*

Some may object to the use of the word "imagination" in describing these events. Their objections are understandable, because our imagination, like all our reason, was corrupted by the Fall. But just as our reason can be redeemed, so can our imagination be renewed.

The use of the imagination in Christian meditation is not seeing things that are *not* real and wishing them into existence. Rather, it is seeing things that *are* real: Abraham's "city that has foundations," Stephen's vision of Jesus standing by the throne, the New Jerusalem continuously coming down out of heaven. The gift of imagination enables us to see things with the eyes of faith and even to have visions from the Lord.

The great Scottish preacher Alexander Whyte spoke of "the divine offices and the splendid services of the Christian imagination.[7] Richard Foster speaks of imagination as a help "to anchor our thoughts and center our attention." He further says that we must seek to think God's thoughts, to delight in His presence, to desire His truth and His ways. "The more we live in this way," he says, "the more God utilizes our imagination for His good purposes."[8]

Imagination leads to understanding the Word of God.

Constructive Bible study would be impossible without using the imagination God has given us. Without imagination how could we envision John's heavenly city with streets of gold and the river of life flowing through it?

More importantly, how could we understand Jesus and His ministry without using this precious gift of imagination? He is at one and the same time my Savior, King, Friend, Lord, Bridegroom, Suffering Servant, Elder Brother, Baby in a manger, Healer, Teacher, Vine, God's Eternal Wisdom, the Lily of the Valley, the Bright Morning Star, the Shepherd, the Judge of all humankind; and He is the Lover of my soul!

Imagination enables the Bible student to read not only with his head, to understand concepts and ideas, but also with his heart, so that he might enter into worship and divine communion with the Lord. C. S. Lewis stated it best when he said, "While reason is the natural organ of truth, imagination is the organ of meaning."[9] Well into the Middle Ages the Bible was read in the monasteries not simply to understand doctrine but "so that one could step into it, find it's meaning inwardly and be transformed."[10]

Throughout the centuries, God's people have captured the imagery of the Scriptures by using their God-given gift of imagination. Michelangelo "liberated" David from a block of stone; Charles Wesley called the Church to worship through his mighty hymns. George Friedrich Handel interpreted the Scripture's revelation of messianic teaching through his *Messiah*, far surpassing any commentator's attempts at verbal explanation. Rembrandt "painted" the suffering, compassionate heart of God in his *Return of the Prodigal Son*. All these saw, through their God-given gift of imagination, things that were real, but which could be seen only with the eyes of faith and not with reason alone.

Everyone is born with imagination! We all possess it and are called by God to use our imagination to create with Him! And meditation on the Word of God is greatly enhanced through the proper use of sanctified imagination.

Imagination leads to faith.

I met Apollo at a joint retreat for students from Duke University, the University of North Carolina and North Carolina State University. He quickly informed me that many other students were praying for his salvation. But he didn't seem to mind. In fact, he appreciated their expressions of love and concern. As a Chinese-American he enjoyed the interracial, international flavor of the Christian community there.

But the weekend was coming to a close with still no breakthrough for Apollo. Holy Communion was planned for the last evening together, following the Bible teaching. But as I was finishing the exposition of God's Word, I noticed that the communion elements had not been placed on the altar. The student in charge had forgotten to make preparations, and all we had was a table covered with a beautiful white cloth! How could we conduct the service of the Lord's Supper without the bread and wine?

Then I remembered. Years before, when The Rev. Francis MacNutt came to Korea to teach the Church about the healing ministry and to try to restore the ministry of healing to the Church, I served as his interpreter. As was mentioned in a previous chapter, God performed many remarkable healings during these weeks together.

Holy Communion was planned for the last morning of the workshop. The Rev. MacNutt, who at the time was a Dominican priest, gave the invitation to all the 800 or more participants, Protestant and Catholic, to partake together as a sign of our unity in Jesus Christ. My heart was warmed and hopeful as I stood beside him and gave the invitation in the Korean language.

But we were soon disappointed as another Roman Catholic priest rushed to the podium to announce briskly that this was a Catholic Mass and would the Protestants please refrain from partaking. Filled with anger and frustration I took my seat, choosing a chair far away near a corner of the back wall.

As I sat there feeling sorry for myself, Someone came to visit me. Jesus Himself appeared to me, not in a visibly physical form, but still as real as the people around me. God was using the vehicle of my imagination to reveal Himself to me.

Jesus asked me if I would like to receive communion. "Yes, Lord, I really want to partake of your body and blood, but it is impossible now," I replied. Jesus then administered the communion to me, " . . . This is My body, broken for you . . . this cup is the new covenant in My blood, shed for you. Take it and eat."

An elderly nun walked slowly towards my seat, just as I was finishing my "mystical" communion. With tears in her eyes, she said, "I'm truly sorry you couldn't partake with us, but nobody told me I couldn't share what I received with you." She drew her hand from behind her back and gave me the remaining half of her wafer the priest had given to her. And I partook of the Holy Communion the second time that morning!

Now, years later, as I stood before the empty Communion Table before the large group of university students, I had the solution. "Please feel free to come up and kneel at the altar. You will see that the Communion Table is empty. But we will ask Jesus Himself to come and administer the loaf and the cup to you, if you will come in faith."

And they came. I stepped aside, wondering if perhaps I had misused or at least slightly stretched the use of imagination with the students. I began to think of how these may be the intelligentsia of tomorrow, and how this could turn out to be a very embarrassing situation for all of us. Until I turned and saw scores of students rushing to the front, all kneeling before the altar, some with their faces nearly to the floor.

There was Apollo, right at the very front of the altar. His lips were moving; he seemed to be praying; he even seemed to be eating and drinking! Apollo was actually partaking of Holy Communion, and Jesus was the one serving him!

Later, during a time of testimonies after the meeting, Apollo came up to the front. He thanked everyone for praying for him so diligently and announced that tonight he had given his life to Jesus Christ and accepted Him as his Lord and Savior. "When Jesus fed me the bread and then the cup, and when He said to me, 'Apollo, here, take and eat. I have been waiting for you,' I knew right then that He was calling me out of the rule and powers of darkness into His kingdom of light. And I gave Him my life; I will live only for Him!"

Imagination! This powerful gift from God led young Apollo to "see" God, to have a spiritual encounter with Jesus Christ meaningful enough to allow him to commit his life to God and to confess that he would live his future life only for Him!

Imagination personalizes the Word of God.

Imagination is a powerful tool for meditating on the Word of God. It is that key that enables us to personalize the Word of God as we meditate on it. At times this valuable gift enables us to bring to reality an experience of the past: to "relive" the disciples' walk along the Emmaus road and so to meet Jesus who appeared to them and now appears to us; to sit with Jesus and the woman of Samaria as He leads her to become a worshiper of the Father and now calls again to us to worship the Father in Spirit and in truth.

We can meditate together effectively by group role-playing. Even children can join in with adults in acting out a parable from the Gospels, an incident in the life of Jesus, or a story from the Old Testament. We should begin by asking the Holy Spirit to guide each person's use of imagination. Then, as we relive the incident, we will be deeply touched as the Spirit opens the deep truths of Scripture by using our imagination.

At other times the proper use of imagination enables us to grasp with more intensity a present experience, to meet the Good Shepherd today as He appears to us and leads, protects, and feeds us. Imagination makes the printed word of the biblical text come alive, as the Holy Spirit of God plants it inside our innermost being to bear fruit for the Lord.

There are still other times when imagination allows us to enter into the future and taste beforehand an event yet to be experienced. None of us have experienced that perfect solitude, peace and incomparable joy that awaits us in heaven, but every time we enter into the Holy of Holies to meet our Savior, our imagination is hard at work as a tool of the Holy Spirit to give us a foretaste of that peace and joy even now. Ellen and I share a heart to know and love the people of North Korea more deeply and to share God's grace and goodness with them. We have not yet been able to fully enter into this joy, but we can taste it; we can actually experience it in our hearts, because of this great gift of imagination.

The Danger of Self-Centered Fantasy

But isn't imagination dangerous? Will it not lead us into all sorts of evil fantasies and into a lifestyle that is far from reality? Yes, this is possible. Fantasy that results from an idle, lazy and undisciplined mind can be dangerous and detrimental to the person using it, as well as to those who are affected by it. On the other hand, fantasy that is the result of disciplined minds wholly committed to glorifying God produces fruit that honors God, as we can see in the literary works of George MacDonald, or in C. S. Lewis' *Chronicles of Narnia* or J. R. R. Tolkien's *Lord of the Rings*.

God's Spirit desires to use our imagination as His tool to lead us into true vision, to be men and women of vision. Unfortunately too often we become people of unhealthy fantasy. Self-centered fantasy is the improper use of the imagination that God gave us to create with Him. It is a cancer that spreads in the mind and heart and, like physical cancer, will lead to death if not removed.

When a person enters the world of fantasy for selfish indulgence, the result is disorientation that leads to a distortion of reality. This is an improper use of imagination. Vision, on the other hand, is the fruit of imagination that allows one to see beyond the visible into the unseen reality. Self-centered fantasy is unattainable; the seeker never finds the object. Vision leads to fulfillment of faith and realization of God's plan.

Most people engage in self-centered fantasy at some time. They dream of winning the lottery and becoming an instant millionaire. They see themselves in a dreamy world where they instantly, without gifts or discipline, become a famous operatic diva or a painter whose works rival Raphael or Van Gogh. Other fantasies can be more dangerous, such as fantasizing about an improper relationship with a person of the opposite sex. King David entertained such fantasies about Bathsheba and nearly destroyed his entire kingdom as well as his relationship with his own household. This kind of fantasy destroys good relationships while focusing on unrealistic or improper relationships.

Self-centered fantasy closes the door to God's influence and opens the door to Satan's control over our lives. Events at the close of the 20th century in North America showed clearly that the Enemy also desires to use the imagination that God gave to us for God's own glory. Two young teenagers who fantasized about what it would be like to take an automatic weapon into their high school and murder all their enemies actually did that very thing. An entire nation was affected because of their evil use of imagination.

What is God's way of overcoming evil fantasies and leading us into a healthy, creative use of the imaginative powers He has given us? Certainly it is not to throw imagination out the door as a "dangerous creature." No, God wants to transform our imagination, renewing it just as He renews our power to reason and to think. Here are some ways to cooperate with God's Spirit as He renews our imagination.

Be filled with the Word of God.

The only way to be renewed in our minds—our thinking, our imagination, our wills, our emotions—is to allow the Word of Christ to dwell within us richly, controlling our every thought and emotion and redirecting them to God Himself. "Let the word of Christ dwell in you richly, teaching and admonishing one another in all wisdom, singing psalms and hymns and spiritual songs, with thankfulness in your hearts to God," declares Paul as he appeals to the Christians of Colossae to allow God to transform them in every area of their lives. (Colossians 3:16-17)

Being filled with the Word of God, soaked in the Word, making our home in the Word, is the important first step in overcoming fantasies and walking in vision. Imagination without discipline brings spiritual death, but imagination used with the disciplines of the Christian faith—prayer, study and meditation on the Word of God, faithfulness and servanthood in community, and diligence in evangelism—opens the door for unlimited potential in serving God.

Repent of evil uses of imagination.

Ask the Holy Spirit to help you recall past misuses and abuses of the gift of imagination. As He brings them to mind, confess them out loud to God and repent of these sins. Turn away from them. Change your mind about their value, realizing that they will destroy you for the sake of a few moments of fleeting pleasure. Turn back to God and receive His cleansing, forgiving grace through the blood of the Lord Jesus Christ. Be free! Let the past be the past. Bury the ashes of past sins and walk in newness, realizing that your imagination has been set free.

Submit your imagination to the Holy Spirit.

Begin to ask God to speak to you. Meditate daily on one verse of Scripture. Pray through each line, word by word, and allow God to reform your imagination with His thoughts, His creative ideas, His vision for the future. Practice obeying the promptings of the Spirit. Set your mind on the things above, on God, rather than things in the world and things below. Refuse to allow Satan to use your imagination for his own sordid, destructive purposes. Take back your imagination from the Enemy and submit it totally to God. Then you will become a man of God who looks to the future with confident expectation, a woman of God who walks with God and whose mind is constantly filled with His presence.

Remember, as you are becoming free, that you can now use your imagination for good and pleasant things and not for evil lust and selfish goals. Know also that when sexual temptations come, you can imagine not only the temporary pleasure they may bring, but, more importantly, you can also imagine the beauty and strength that will come to you as you overcome such temptations in the power of the Holy Spirit. You will discover that imagination is God's gift to free you from selfish ambitions and Satan's attacks and to lead you into a life of great vision for God. You will begin to think great thoughts about God, pray great prayers to God, and attempt great deeds for God.

As you submit your imagination to the Holy Spirit while you meditate daily on the Word of God, you will discover that imagination is a great tool for understanding the Word of God and for entering into the reality of the Bible. You will discover as well that the very act of daily meditation will reward you with a purified imagination, free you from sin and lead you into His abundant life.

The Sixth Tool: Soliloquy

The sixth tool that will aid you in your daily meditation is soliloquy, or "talking to oneself." This is a very helpful tool not only in meditation but also in maintaining a disciplined Christian life. It is very biblical to talk to yourself, especially when you feel depressed or anxious, even angry. Consider the psalmist's words: "Why are you cast down, O my soul, and why are you in turmoil within me? Hope in God; for I shall again praise Him, my salvation and my God!" (Psalm 42:11) Who is doing the talking? I am, and I am talking to my soul and asking myself why I am depressed and in turmoil. Then I exhort my soul to hope in God!

The psalmist encourages us to talk to ourselves: "Bless the Lord, O my soul, and all that is within me, bless His holy name . . . and forget not all His benefits!" (Psalm 103:1-2) At times the psalmist almost seems to equate meditation with soliloquy, as in Psalm 77, when he records the content of his meditation. Notice that here again the psalmist is talking to himself.

> *Let me meditate in my heart. Then my spirit made a diligent search: "Will the Lord spurn forever, and never again be favorable? Has His steadfast love forever ceased? Are His promises at an end for all time? Has God*

*forgotten to be gracious? Has He in anger
shut up His compassion?"* (Psalm 77:6-9)

When you are meditating on a verse of Scripture, repeat the verse over and over until you are familiar with its content. Then, in some instances, you may want to talk to yourself about what the verse says. Suppose you are meditating on the words, "I can do all things through Him who strengthens me." (Philippians 4:13) But today you do not feel strong, rather you feel unable to do anything. So you say to yourself, "I really cannot do anything, I am tired and sometimes I even want to give up. I am not content. Does God understand how weak I really am?" However, you can talk to yourself in another way. You may say to yourself, "I know I can do all that God tells me to do. Soul, don't say you can do nothing, because if you abide in Christ you can do all things! You can be content in plenty or in want. O my soul, you must be strengthened in Him!"

Soliloquy can aid us greatly in meditation. We talk to ourselves just as the psalmist did, exhorting ourselves to be strong by abiding in Him. This becomes the basis for prayer. We begin talking not only to ourselves, but also to God. Remember that to meditate is to have "dialogue" with God. As we continue to talk with God we thank Him that He abides in us in power, that His presence is our strength. We may confess that we have not been abiding in Him and in His Word, receive forgiveness and then commit to abiding in Him as a daily lifestyle. Soliloquy then leads into worship, where we once again present our bodies as a living sacrifice, strengthened to do His will in the world.

Meditation never takes us out of the world of reality but rather causes us to go with Christ more deeply into the sorrows and suffering of the world to be His agents of reconciliation. These six tools will ensure that our meditation is biblical and will increase our ability to be servants to a world in pain.

Invitation to the Banquet Table
Personal Meditation on Psalm 139

1. Review the four simple steps of meditation.
First, prepare your heart.
Second, listen to all God wants to say to you through the
text.
Third, seek to meet God as He reveals Himself to you.
Fourth, respond to Him in prayer and obedience.

2. Read through the entire chapter of Psalm 139.
Open yourself to God and listen as you read.
Try to understand what the psalmist wants to express
through this psalm.

3. Meditate on Psalm 139, **verses 17 and 18.**
How precious to me are your thoughts, O God!
How vast is the sum of them!
If I would count them, they are more than the sand.
I awake, and I am still with you.
God continually thinks about you.
His thoughts about you are filled with love.
He will renew you in that love as you talk with Him.
Ask Him to share His thoughts with you.

Listen to what the Lord wants to say to you personally!

4. Write down in your Meditation Journal what the Lord
says to you.
Or you may write out your prayer to Him.
Allow the Spirit to lead you as you listen to the Lord.

5. Take time now to wait upon the Lord.
Give Him your heart. Ask Him to reveal Himself to you.

6. Spend time in prayer.
Thank God for His word to you.
Commit yourself to obey Him.

Chapter 15

Overcoming Hindrances to Meditation

Meditation on the Word of God is one of the most powerful means of grace that God has given us to maintain communion with Him. Each act of meditation removes the barriers that separate us from Christ. At the very moment that Jesus Christ was crucified on the cross, the curtain of the temple was torn in two, from top to bottom. Christ Himself took upon Himself our separation from God, represented by the temple veil, and provided a new and living way of direct access to the throne of God. Yet because of our sinful nature we still live as though we cannot see Him clearly.

I once went to the Himalayas in Nepal on a "prayer-trekking" mission with a group of students and colleagues. Rising early each morning before daybreak and observing the sun bursting forth upon the snow-covered mountain peaks was a breathtaking experience. But some mornings were cloudy and foggy. All we could see were a few trees in front of us. We were standing before the most majestic mountain peaks in the world, yet we could not see them.

So it is with our relationship with God. God is always before us; He walks beside us. But we do not always see Him.

Each morning when we meditate, the fog gradually lifts and we see Him more clearly. We enter His presence more fully. We experience the promise of Solomon, who said, "But the path of the righteous is like the light of dawn, which shines brighter and brighter until full day." (Proverbs 4:18)

But there are hindrances to meditation. Some are obvious and need only discipline to correct. We often experience difficulties in meditation because we do not meditate on a regular basis. Sporadic meditation will more likely lead to frustration than to peace of mind. We must meditate daily, insofar as possible. Other difficulties come when we are not obedient to the word God has spoken to us. How can we expect Him to continue to speak if we ignore the commands He has already given us? We must hasten to obey all that He says to us.

Another hindrance is discouragement at not seeing immediate results. Meditation is a process, and it will lead us to bear fruit. But good fruit does not grow quickly. At times others cannot see the fruit in our lives, and we become disappointed at the lack of recognition. But a true meditator, one who truly contemplates as a lifestyle, knows that meditation is hard work, and even when the meditator does not feel a strong excitement or satisfaction, he continues to trust God that He will be faithful. My mother was a master seamstress, one who put all her love into every garment she made. Most of her customers, although deeply satisfied, never noticed nor acknowledged the hours of labor and painstaking care she put into her work. But she never became discouraged, because she was working "as to the Lord." Ellen's father was a professor of Bible at a Christian college. His students loved and respected him, but few of them knew the long, laborious hours he poured into his study and preparation, using his knowledge and creativity to glorify God. Most of the time this "labor of love" went unnoticed by his students. Yet he was not discouraged, because he was serving the Lord and was committed to glorifying Him each day of his life. Is this not the heart of a meditator?

One of the most commonly experienced hindrances to meditation is the inability to concentrate. Wandering thoughts, even sinful thoughts, often attack the meditator. Satan is very much afraid of a committed Christian who meditates daily on God's Word and seeks to glorify Him through his obedience. So he attempts to distract him. Sometimes he will cause us to have wandering thoughts. At other times he will bring to our memory *his own* negative thoughts that he has planted in us over the years, or memories of unfortunate or tragic circumstances we have encountered. God wants us to remember His faithfulness, but Satan tempts us to remember our wounds and past sorrows. When negative memories become a serious problem in meditation we should seek help from the Body of Christ. Christ has given gifts of healing to His Church, and when we pray for the healing of troublesome memories, His Spirit removes them, cleanses us and protects us from the damage they would cause.

Whether the hindrance is simply straying thoughts, or the inability to concentrate, here are some practical suggestions that will help us maintain fellowship with God through meditation.

Relax. We should not be worried or shocked if we experience these difficulties. Remember! We live in a noise-based culture, so we should not be surprised that at times when we wish to be silent an "inner riot" almost breaks out within us. We simply must remain calm, be patient and persevere. God understands that we are but dust, and that we need help. And He has promised that we can come boldly before His throne at any and all times, to receive His grace in time of need. We must remember also to *focus* on the text itself. If we cannot concentrate, we can stand up and read it aloud. We should read it as many times as we need to regain our concentration. Or we can relax by going outside and taking a walk. We can read other passages of the Scriptures. We will find that our minds are again at peace; the inner noise will begin to fade. And we will hear our Lord speaking to us.

Resist. When necessary we must resist Satan and his demonic angels in the mighty name of Jesus Christ. Martin Luther taught us to sing, "One little word (Jesus) will fell him (Satan)!" Jesus drove out the moneychangers and pigeon sellers from the temple, telling them to get out and stop making His Father's house a marketplace. We must remember that *we are now* the "Father's house," and we must let these words of Christ rest in our hearts. We can ask Christ to command the distractions to go away, to drive them out just as He did long ago in Palestine. We must not let the Enemy's distractions stop us from entering into the throne room of God, for "He who is in us is greater than he who is in the world!" (1 John 4:4) We must use the weapons at our disposal to confront the enemy, refusing to allow him to block our access to God.

Alison Oliver, who was a faithful meditator on God's Word, wrote this brief poem after she meditated on the story of David and Goliath:

Eclipsed by the giant
In the shadows I tremble.

Where is my sword?
Where is my shield?

I search,
Only to find
Within my hands
A simple slingshot
And a stone . . .
Ah, victory is near! [1]

Remove. We must remove the things that oppress us and drag us down. "Let us lay aside every weight, and sin which clings so closely," says the writer to the Hebrews. (Hebrews 12:1) After we have resisted Satan, we then can shake off the things that hold us back and interrupt our times of meditation and contemplation, whether they are worries or anxieties, or feelings of sadness or loneliness. We deal with the sins "which cling so closely" by confessing them to God, repenting and receiving His forgiveness. This will once again open the channels of communication with God.

Resume. After we have done these three things, we then resume our meditation. "Lift your drooping hands and strengthen your weak knees, and make straight paths for your feet, so that what is lame may not be put out of joint but rather be healed." (Hebrews 12:12-13) We can indeed do all things through Christ who lives within us. His Spirit desires to draw us closer to the Lord. God even sends his angels to help us in time of need.

Above all, do not be afraid of times of barrenness, or aridity of spirit. Every meditator will experience at some time the "dark night of the soul," as St. John of the Cross described it. "We must be prepared to experience the dark night to some degree," writes von Balthasar. "It is a sign that [we] are on the path of Christ, i.e., it is a sign of consolation, even though it is bound to take the form of a withdrawal of consolation."[2] We must remember that God is in control and He will lead us through this valley. We can use these times as an opportunity for purification of the soul, for removing all things in our lives that seek to replace Jesus Christ as the only Lord of our lives. The Spirit is ready to help us as we turn to Him.

Invitation to the Banquet Table
Personal Meditation on Psalm 139

1. Review the four simple steps of meditation.
First, prepare your heart.
Second, listen to all God wants to say to you through the
text.
Third, seek to meet God as He reveals Himself to you.
Fourth, respond to Him in prayer and obedience.

2. Read through the entire chapter of Psalm 139.
Open yourself to God and listen as you read.
Try to understand what the psalmist wants to express
through this psalm.

3. Meditate on Psalm 139, **verses 19-22.**
Oh that you would slay the wicked, O God!
O men of blood, depart from me!
They speak against you with malicious intent; your enemies
take your name in vain!
Do I not hate those who hate you, O Lord?
And do I not loathe those who rise up against you?
I hate them with complete hatred; I count them my
enemies.

Remember that Satan is the great Enemy of God.
Receive God's strength to oppose all demonic powers and principalities.
Realize, too, that we must oppose evil persons who oppose God
and who cause other people to live lives of debasement, without dignity.
Ask God how He wants you to pray for evil people in the world.
Listen to what the Lord wants to say to you personally!

4. Write down in your Meditation Journal what the Lord says to you.
Or you may write out your prayer to Him.
Allow the Spirit to lead you as you listen to the Lord.

5. Take time now to wait upon the Lord.
Give Him your heart. Ask Him to reveal Himself to you.

6. Spend time in prayer.
Thank God for His word to you.
Commit yourself to obey Him.

Chapter 16

The Act of Meditation

We have begun our journey of meditation, a journey that will lead us into the unsurpassed joy of ever increasing communion with our Lord. The method for meditation is simple and can be easily learned. We have spoken of the method in the preface to this book, and you have nearly completed your meditation on Psalm 139. Now we must look more closely at *how* to meditate.

Various Ways to Meditate

There are many ways to meditate on the Scriptures. You should seek to learn and practice the method that is best suited to you, and not try to follow someone else's way of doing it. Meditation on stories of the Bible is an effective way to meditate. Read through stories such as that of David and Goliath, the Good Samaritan, Jesus and the woman of Samaria, or the Elijah and Elisha stories. As you read the story, observe what each person is saying or doing, as well as the context or situation. Do not be satisfied to merely understand the story with your mind, but personalize the story by "entering into" the situation. Sit at the well beside Jesus and the Samaritan woman. Stand beside David as he faces insurmountable odds in battle. Stay with Elijah as he sits under the broom tree, depressed and asking God to take his life, all this after he has just won a magnificent battle with evil forces. Become a part of these stories, make them your own, and God will speak to you through them.

Another form of meditation is to ponder the concepts or ideas that are central to the Gospel story, such as the blood of Jesus, God's love shown by His sacrifice of His Son on the Cross, or the Suffering Servant. You may use a concordance to find key verses that describe these important ideas. Then go through these verses one by one and ask God to speak through them. George Frederic Handel (1685-1759), who composed the *Messiah,* was a meditator. Simple observation reveals that the content of this masterpiece consists simply of verses of Scripture that speak of the Messiah, or of the salvation we have in Christ. Handel must have searched the Scriptures diligently to examine these verses. Then he spent time meditating on each one of them, asking God to reveal Himself through the Word, to speak to him about the Messiah. The result is a work of art composed in the 18th century that still continues into the 21st century to move the hearts of men and women and draw them to the Messiah, Jesus Christ!

An effective way to meditate on Scripture is to choose an individual such as Joseph, or Enoch, Elijah or Mary the mother of Jesus, or Mary of Bethany. This form of meditation provides rich insights into the mind and heart of the individual. Often reading other books about these individuals will help your meditating on them. Thomas Mann wrote a classic work on Joseph, fictional but scripturally based.[1] The well-known Brazilian author Paulo Coelho has produced a deeply penetrating novel about Elijah.[2] Other reference books or commentaries will be helpful as you study Bible personalities. You will see yourself in these people as God speaks to you about them. Remember, though, that your meditation must be on the Bible itself, and not books about the Bible or on other people's descriptions of these fascinating individuals.

There are many methods of Bible meditation. Perhaps you have developed your own method. But as we pointed out in the preface to this book, great numbers of Christians throughout the long history of the Church have discovered that *no method is more powerful and effective than meditating verse-by-verse, one or two verses a day, through passages of the Bible!* God will reveal Himself to you. He will meet you each day, as you enter His presence. And you will be transformed.

The First Thing to Do

First of all, choose the passage on which you will meditate. You may wish to meditate on a psalm. If this is the case, pray and ask God to bring to your mind the psalm He would like to give you for meditation. Or you may already have a psalm that is dear to your heart, and on which you would like to spend time meditating, verse-by-verse. Those who have meditated on Psalm 119 (all 176 verses!) give powerful witness to the way God has given them an entirely new love for the Word of God through meditating on this psalm!

Paul's letters offer excellent material on which to meditate. Choose one of Paul's shorter letters such as Philippians, Colossians or Ephesians. First, read the whole letter through. Then begin with chapter one, verse one (do not begin in the middle of the book) and proceed through the letter a verse a day. Or you may choose a favorite chapter of the Bible that has special meaning for you. For example, if you meditate through Isaiah chapters forty through sixty-six (each chapter) you will meet Jesus, the Suffering Servant, in a fresh way, and you will be greatly encouraged by the treasures to be unearthed there.

You have nearly completed your meditation on Psalm 139. *Take time now to pray and ask God to help you decide on your next Scripture for meditation.* Where will you begin?

Review of the Four Simple Steps for Effective Bible Meditation

Your effectiveness as a Bible meditator will continue to grow if you develop your own personal method of meditation. Try to avoid formal, legalistic ways of meditation that will consume your time but not feed your soul. God wants to speak to *you, personally.* You are capable of hearing Him. He is your Father. You are His child. He delights in you! He is your Shepherd, you are one of His sheep; and all His sheep know His voice. He is your Master; you are His servant. The Master will always speak to you, because you are His servant. He knows that you need to know His will in order to obey it. He is the Lover of your soul and He desires to whisper His words to you in your time of intimacy with Him.

Let's review the four simple steps that we suggested in the beginning of this book. They are intended to enable you to begin your life of meditation. God will bless you as you begin!

Step One: Prepare

Preparation is very important. Prepare your body. Sit in a comfortable chair (but not so comfortable that it makes you go to sleep), or take a stroll as you meditate. One of the definitions of the word *meditate* is "to stroll." Prepare your spirit to meditate. Remember that God has invited you to come into His presence! You are not inviting God. He is inviting you! Jesus chose His disciples for three reasons: that *they might be with Him,* that He might send them out to preach, and that He might give them authority to cast out demons. (Mark 3:13-15) God desires to meet you; He welcomes you into His presence each morning, so that you can be with Him throughout your day's journey.

Prepare your heart to meet Him. Psalm 139:23-24 is a good prayer to pray as you make sure your heart is right with God:

> *Search me, O God, and know my heart!*
> *Try me and know my thoughts!*
> *And see if there be any grievous way in me,*
> *And lead me in the way everlasting!*

Confess any sins that God reveals to you and receive forgiveness before you meditate on His Word. Unconfessed sin will lead only to confusion and lack of understanding. You may pray also the psalmist's prayer in Psalm 119:18, " Open my eyes, that I may behold wondrous things out of Your law." Open yourself to God and to His Word.

Step Two: Listen

The second step is to *listen.* Listening is the key to all fruitful meditation. Making time to listen to God is essential for discipleship. Former United Nations Secretary General Dag Hammarskjold once remarked, "How can you expect to keep your powers of hearing when you never want to listen? That God should have time for you, you seem to take as much for granted as that you cannot have time for Him." How true this is! By now, however, you will have made the big decision: you will make time each day, before the rush of activity that comes upon you like a flood, to listen to God in His Word.

Remember, this is God's Word *to you, personally*. You do not have to share this word immediately with anyone, because it is your own word directly from God. Read the verse over and over, and God's Spirit will cause these precious words to enter your heart and your spirit, as well as your mind. Use the tools that you have learned. Observe what the text says. Repeat the words over and over in your mind, or out loud. Use your imagination. But above all, *listen.* Three keys to listening are: *Wait, Wait, Wait!* Dialogue with God is not possible until you wait upon Him and listen to what He has to say to you. *Expect* Him to speak. Your joy will be made complete, when you hear the words that He wants to speak to you each morning!

Step Three: Meet

Do not stop your meditation after you have heard God speak to you. Continue to listen, and you will discover that the words God is speaking to you, in fact the very words of the Scripture upon which you are meditating, will lead you into the presence of God! Take time to meet Him! Ask Him to reveal Himself to you. Madame Guyon (1648-1717), a French mystic acclaimed by Christians throughout the world as a saint who experienced God through prayer, said, *"Hold your heart in His presence!"* Give God your heart. No one other than God has first claim to your heart! Lift your heart to him, through the words of Scripture on which you are meditating, and say to Him that you greatly desire to meet Him. Moses asked to see God, and God replied to him, "Behold, there is a place by Me." (Exodus 33:21) God has reserved a place directly by Him, and this place is for *you!* Your joy will be made full in His presence, as you meet Him and gaze upon His magnificent beauty and behold His glory.

This is the point when meditation leads into contemplation. We have sought God as we meditated on His Word, listening to all that He desired to say to us. Now is the time of celebration, the time of great joy because we see Him as He reveals Himself to us.

Many Christians have not experienced the joy of resting in the presence of the Lord, of sitting before Him not only to listen to His words but also to see Him, to gaze into His wondrous face. Perhaps this will be the beginning for you, and you will be able to walk with Him in greater intimacy, in fuller trust and obedience.

Step Four: Respond

The final step in meditation is to respond to God's speaking to you, and to His meeting you. God intends for His Word always to bring transformation to our lives. And that transformation comes as we respond to Him.

Prayer is always the major response to God in meditation. Thank Him for speaking to you. Pour out your heart of love for Him in prayer. Offer up prayers of confession or intercession for loved ones and for the nations of the world. God's Word will always lead you into prayer.

Keep a Meditation Journal. Each day, write out the verse on which you are meditating. Then, as God speaks to you, write down what He says, so that you won't forget. Sometimes you can write out your own prayer that you prayed to God. Or you can write out ideas and thoughts that come to you while you are meditating. Your Meditation Journal will be a great encouragement to you in the years to come, when you look back and read again the wonderful words your Master spoke to you, and the great thoughts He gave you!

Respond creatively, using the talents God has given to you in music, sketching, painting, dance or other areas. Sing a new song to the Lord, using the words of your Scriptural meditation. At times the only response is to paint a picture or draw a sketch to express your love for God. Perform a creative worship dance on the basis of your time of meeting God. God created the world by His Word! Now He wants to create new history by that same Word, through you as you respond to Him!

Above all, *obey* the word that God has spoken to you. We listen in order to obey, and show our great love for Him by applying that word to our lives through joyful and complete obedience to all He has commanded us to do. The mark of a true meditator, as well as the key to a dynamic Christian life, is listening and obeying. Your spiritual growth will become evident to others, as you walk in obedience to His Word.

You are now ready to become the meditator God desires. Continue to meditate until it becomes your lifestyle. You *desire* to become a meditator like Joshua or like Mary. What remains now is your *determination* to pursue this goal and your *commitment* to be faithful. God will give you strength; He will speak to you and meet you far beyond your expectations. God has blessed you so that you can become a blessing to others. Teach another person to meditate. Use the materials provided for you in this book and help at least one other person to enter this exciting new world of Bible meditation.

Invitation to the Banquet Table
Personal Meditation on Psalm 139

1. Review the four simple steps of meditation.
First, prepare your heart.
Second, listen to all God wants to say to you through the
text.
Third, seek to meet God as He reveals Himself to you.
Fourth, respond to Him in prayer and obedience.

2. Read through the entire chapter of Psalm 139.
Open yourself to God and listen as you read.
Try to understand what the psalmist wants to express
through this psalm.

3. Meditate on Psalm 139, **verses 23-24.**
Search me, O God, and know my heart!
Try me and know my thoughts! And see if there be any
grievous way in me,
And lead me in the way everlasting!
God has opened His heart to you, as you have meditated on
this psalm.
Now, open your heart to God.
Ask the Spirit to search your heart and reveal what He sees.

Pray this prayer with the psalmist.
Listen to what the Lord wants to say to you personally!

4. Write down in your Meditation Journal what the Lord
says to you.
Or you may write out your prayer to Him.
Allow the Spirit to lead you as you listen to the Lord.

5. Take time now to wait upon the Lord.
Give Him your heart. Ask Him to reveal Himself to you.

6. Spend time in prayer.
Thank God for His word to you.
Commit yourself to obey Him.

*You have now
come to the end of your
meditation on Psalm 139. Consider the
great things God has done for you as you
have meditated.
Write out a prayer of thanksgiving
to God for His grace and
faithfulness.*

*Now, choose the next passage for
your meditation.*

A Word In Closing

M editation is a lost art. Perhaps it would be more accurate to say that it is a lost jewel in the crown of the
Christian. One thing we can say with certainty is that meditation is a rich treasure that needs to be rediscovered by the
people of God. The men and women God used mightily in
the Scriptures were all meditators.

The Early church continued to emphasize the importance and power of meditation during those dynamic years
of the first and second centuries when the Church grew and
conquered spiritually the entire Roman Empire. Even during
the period when the Church became secularized by will-
ingly accepting the privileges of power and wealth under
the Emperor Constantine in the fourth century, the Desert
Fathers kept meditation and contemplation alive. In fact,
their instruction on meditation is a rich source for those who
seek to be meditators today.

Every century has had its meditators. God's list contains
many well known Church leaders as well as countless saints
whose names are not known by historians but who made an
impact on their age by the power and insight they received
from meditation and by their lives that revealed the fruit of
communion with the Lord.

Add *your* name now to God's list of meditators! Expect God to speak to you and meet you daily. Trust Him to cause the fruit of your meditation to influence the nations of the world.

We invite you to share your experiences in meditation on God's Word, so that Christians of every nation can see *practically* how Biblical meditation can transform their lives and equip them for service to the Lord. We encourage you to write in and share your experiences from meditation. You may write about how meditation has changed your life, or you may share your own method of Bible meditation, or some results, or fruit, of your meditation. Many people will be blessed by your testimony.

You may refer to the website of Antioch Institute for International Ministries: www.ywam-aiim.org. Or you may write directly to:

The Community of the Holy Fire
13717 Cascadian Way
Everett, Washington, 98208
U.S.A.

AIIM
The Meditating Christian
P.O. Box 778
Monroe, Washington 98272-0778
U.S.A.

Endnotes

A Word In the Beginning
  1. Hans Urs von Balthasar, Prayer (San Francisco: Ignatius Press, 1986), 8
  2. Consider the attitude of John the Baptist in John 3:29
  3. Thomas H. Green, S.J., Opening to God (Notre Dame, IN: Ave Maria Press, 1987), 87
  4. See 1 John 1:1-5. The reader would be helped by reading Dietrich Bonhoeffer's classic book on community, Life Together. Bonhoeffer speaks of the Word of God as being central to Christian community.
  5. Note that he commissioned it to the "choirmaster".
  6. Henri Nouwen, Jesus: A Gospel (Maryknoll, NY: Orbis Books, 2001), 48
  7. Campbell McAlpine, The Practice of Biblical Meditation (London: Marshall, Morgan and Scott, 1981), Foreward

Chapter 1   The Meaning of Meditation
  1. Dietrich Bonhoeffer, Meditating on the Word (Cambridge, MA: Cowley Publications, 1986), 51-52
  2. Bonhoeffer, Meditating on the Word, 19-20
  3. The two key Hebrew words for meditation found in the Old Testament are hagah and siyach.

4. Dietrich Bonhoeffer, Psalms: The Prayer Book of the Bible (Minneapolis: Augsburg Publishing House, 1970), 11-12

5. The reader would perhaps benefit by examining some of the New Testament Greek words denoting meditation, such as phroneo, logizomai, skopeo, melatao and promeletao. This can be done by using a concordance (Strong's Concordance contains the Hebrew and Greek words in English phonetics) or by studying the Greek words directly.

6. Psalm 119:18 "Law" and "whole Word of God" are often used synonymously.

7. Peter Toon, From Mind to Heart (Grand Rapids, MI: Baker Book House, 1987), 18

8. Richard Foster, Celebration of Discipline (San Francisco: Harper and Row, 1988), 20

9. Aryeh Kaplan, Meditation and the Bible (York Beach, Maine: Samuel Weiser, Inc., 1978), 3. Kaplan's work tends to border on mysticism, but his research on biblical terminology is very sound.

10. Aryeh Kaplan, Meditation and the Bible, 103-105.

11. Luke 24:30 The story is contained in Luke 24:13-35.

12. Campbell McAlpine, The Practice of Biblical Meditation, 75

13. Campbell McAlpine, 81

14. Peter Toon, Meditating As A Christian (London: Collins, 1991), 161-162

15. The three basic steps of inductive Bible study are: observation, interpretation and application. This effective approach to Bible study is easily learned.

16. Peter Toon, Meditating As A Christian (London: Collins, 1991), 161-162

17. John Michael Talbot, The Fire of Illumination (publisher unknown), 108-109

18. Thomas Merton, Bread In the Wilderness, 14

19. Walter C. Kaiser, former president of Gordon-Conwell
    Theological Seminary

Chapter 2   Seven Keys to Becoming A Meditator
  1. Hans Urs von Balthasar, Prayer (San Francisco: Ignatius
     Press, 182)
  2. Hans Urs von Balthasar, Prayer, 8
  3. Thomas H. Green, S.J., Opening to God (Notre Dame,
     Indiana: Ave Maria Press, 1987)
  4. Hans Urs von Balthasar, Prayer, 22
  5. Hans Urs von Balthasar, Prayer, 7
  6. New Jerusalem Bible translation
  7. Peter Toon, From Mind to Heart, 10
  8. Thomas Merton, Bread In the Wilderness, 60
  9. Thomas Merton, Bread In the Wilderness, 61

Chapter 3   Solitude, Silence and the Word
  1. Genesis 5:24   The biblical data concerning Enoch is
     very sparse, so we must speculate to arrive at the truth
     about him. Nevertheless, it is clear that he enjoyed a very
     intimate relationship with God.
  2. Henri Nouwen, The Way of the Heart (San Francisco:
     Harper & Row, Publishers, 1981) A careful reading of
     this short book will acquaint the reader with a basic
     understanding of solitude.
  3. Nouwen, The Way of the Heart, 23
  4. Nouwen, The Way of the Heart, 20-25
  5. Andrew Murray, The Holiest of All (Old Tappan, NJ:
     Fleming H. Revell Company), 355-356
  6. Catholic Authors, Tales of A Magic Monastery (New
     York: The Crossroad Publishing Co., 1981), p. 55

Chapter 4   The Subject of Our Meditation
  1. Ephesians 3:19, Psalm 16:8, Acts 2:25
  2. Psalm 119:148, 23-24, 54, 111

3. Written by Mary Artemesia Lathbury, 1877
4. The most important resource is the Bible, but there are many helpful books, such as J.I. Packer's Knowing God or T. Layton Fraser's The Christian Life (soon to be revised and published), as well as other theological books.
5. J. I. Packer, Knowing God (Downers Grove, IL: InterVarsity Press), 20
6. It is a good idea to prepare a notebook or journal in which we can write out Bible verses and passages that describe God's character, as well as our observations about God's character, as we read through the Scriptures.
7. Psalm 145: 4-5, 10, 12
8. Read through the songs of The Revelation and notice their references to the blood.
9. Rev. J. Walton Stewart was a pastor with a genuine heart for youth and a vision that inspired them, and this church camp—Camp Stewart—was later named after him.
10. George MacDonald, The Baron's Apprenticeship (Minneapolis: Bethany House Publishers, 1986), 82 (originally published as There and Back, 1891). C.S. Lewis considered George MacDonald to be a major influence in his life and writings.
11. Quoted from Thomas Merton's Journal from Daily Dig (HYPERLINK "http://www.Bruderhof.com/"www. Bruderhof.com) The Daily Dig has now been discontinued.
12. Quoted in The Washington Post, July 30, 1993

Chapter 5 The Seed Is the Word
1. Telegraph of London, March 20, 2003
2. Bonhoeffer, Meditating On the Word, 2
3. See Andrew Murray, The New Life: Words for Young Disciples, at HYPERLINK "http://www.ccel.org/m/murray/"www.ccel.org/m/murray/

Chapter 6   Planting the Seed Through Daily Meditation
 1. Isaiah 42:1-4 (or 42:1-9); 49:1-7; 50:4-9; 52:13-53:12
 2. Dorothy Sayers, The Mind of the Maker (London: Mowbray, 1994), ix
 3. Isaiah 50:4, New Revised Standard Version

Chapter 7   The Faith-Awakening Word
 1. Refer to Joshua 14:5-15 for the story of Caleb's conquest of Hebron.
 2. Hans Urs von Balthasar, Prayer, 16
 3. Augustine, Inarr. in Ps. 118, XXVI, 6. Quoted by Hans Urs von Balthasar, Prayer, 24-25
 4. Numbers chapter 14 gives an account of Moses' intercession.

Chapter 8   Receiving the Seed of God
 1. Ignacio Larranaga, The Silence of Mary (Boston: St. Paul Books and Media, 1991). This widely read Spanish classic gives penetrating insights into the life of Mary.
 2. Ignacio Larranaga, The Silence of Mary, 76
 3. Luke 2:51 New Jerusalem Bible
 4. Henri Nouwen, Jesus, A Gospel (Maryknoll, NY: Orbis Books, 2001), 16
 5. Robert Durback, editor, Seeds of Hope: A Henri Nouwen Reader (New York: Doubleday, Image, 1997), 165-166
 6. Soul Food was written on May 9, 1841.

Chapter 9   The Healing Word
 1. Psalm 139:13-14 New Jerusalem Bible
 2. Jeremiah 1:5 New Jerusalem Bible
 3. The Suffering Church, that is, Christians living under oppressive political regimes, often do not have access to Bibles. In such cases the Spirit ministers directly through increased signs and wonders, through bringing to memory Scripture passages learned earlier before persecution, or

by providing the Word of God to believers in supernatural ways. Yet we must remember that for the Christian living with political freedom who desires to grow, there is no substitute for the Bible. Genuine Christian spirituality never goes beyond the Word of God.
  4. Harvard Business Review, July 1974

Chapter 10 The Restoring Word
  1. This is not her actual name.
  2. Note that Colossians 3:16 is plural, indicating that Paul considered it necessary not only for individuals but also for the whole community to dwell in the Word of God.
  3. Bonhoeffer, Meditation On the Word of God, 133
  4. From notes on Bruce Waltke and Gordon Fee's lectures on Biblical Theology at Regent College, Vancouver, B.C., Canada

Chapter 11 The Sin-Destroying Word
  1. See chapter 9.
  2. Acts chapter 5
  3. Acts chapter 6
  4. Read Psalm 51.

Chapter 12 The Conquering Word
  1. Reading through the Pentateuch and then through the Book of Joshua reveals both the rebellious nature of God's people and their transformation into an obedient people.
  2. Bonhoeffer, Meditating On the Word, 107-108
  3. Deuteronomy 33:3 NASB
  4. Joshua 8:30-35; Deuteronomy 11:26-32
  5. Judy and her husband, Ron Smith, are the international directors of Youth With A Mission's School of Biblical Studies.

Chapter 13   The Fruitful Word
1. See chapter 12 for a discussion of the phrase "law of God."
2. Focusing on each word of the Biblical text is more satisfying if one is using an "essentially literal" translation such as the ESV, NASB, RSV, KJV, NKJV, NRSV. If one is using a "thought-for-thought" translation such as the NIV or NJB, it would be better to focus on the verse as a whole rather than on individual words.
3. John Eaton, The Psalms (London: The Continuum International Publishing Company, 2005), 62
4. It would be helpful to read Jeremiah 23:18-32
5. Excerpts from King Sejong's Yong-bi-eocheon-ga

Chapter 14   Tools for Meditation
1. George MacDonald, The Baron's Apprenticeship, 247
2. Refer to their website at HYPERLINK ""www.thetaizé-community.org
3. Songs from Taizé, Venite Exultemus, recorded in 2001, is available at most music stores.
4. Toon, Meditating As A Christian, 135
6. Hebrews 11:1, New Jerusalem Bible
5. Alister McGrath, Redemption (Minneapolis, MN: Fortress Press, 2006), 62
7. Richard J. Foster, Celebration of Discipline (San Francisco: Harper & Row, Publishers, 1988), 25
8. Foster, 25-26
9. Alister McGrath, 62
10. Morton T. Kelsey, The Other Side of Silence (New York: Paulist Press, 1976), 210

Chapter 15   Hindrances to Meditation
1. Alison Oliver was a vibrant, enthusiastic disciple of Jesus Christ, a faithful missionary who ministered in more than 22 nations, and an excellent Bible teacher.

The Lord called her home to be with Him on August 26, 2004, at the age of 32. God always came first in Alison's life, and she lived her life fully for Him with no regrets. All who knew her loved her and still love and honor her memory.

2. Hans Urs von Balthasar, Prayer, 273

Chapter 16   The Act of Meditation
  1. Thomas Mann, Joseph In Egypt (New York: Alfred A. Knopf, Inc., 1938)
  2. Paulo Coelho, The Fifth Mountain (New York: HarperCollins Publishers, Inc., 1998)

Printed in the United States
201855BV00001B/1-93/A

9 781602 662063